WIMBLEDON 1877–1977

WIMBLEDON
1877–1977

MAX
ROBERTSON

ARTHUR BARKER LIMITED LONDON
A subsidiary of Weidenfeld (Publishers) Ltd

CONTENTS

ILLUSTRATIONS

LP = © Arthur Cole and Le-Roye
    Productions
BN = © Beaverbrook Newspapers Ltd

TO THE CHAMPIONSHIPS
AND ALL WHO PLAY THEIR PART IN THEM

Rain on Ladies Final day
Centre Court, Friday 6 July 1973

The British are a patient lot,
God wot.
On the Centre Court they stand and stare
At the ghosts of players who are not there
And grin and bear
Their lot.

They've queued all night, they've stood all day,
So they have to stay –
To endorse the ardour they've all displayed
'Til the decision, so long delayed,
Gives rain again the Final say –
Call it a day.

FOREWORD

An event of such importance as the hundredth anniversary of Wimbledon will undoubtedly bring forth many books and pictorials.

When the writer of such a book is Max Robertson, it bears the stamp of authority and an insider's perspective. Since the war, Max Robertson has been the voice of the BBC. His play-by-play commentaries and word pictures of actual events have carried the aura of this magnificent spectacle into millions of homes all over the world. It has been my good fortune to work closely with him during many Wimbledons. His knowledge of players and spectacular descriptions of matches never cease to amaze me. Who better than Max Robertson to write the story that appears in these pages?

For the player, Wimbledon has become the pinnacle of achievement. For the spectators who endlessly wait in queues overnight to gain admission for the following day's matches, and for those who breathlessly send for their tickets in the cold of January, it is a 'must'.

For me, it is Wimbledon . . . and that says it all. No other name carries the mystique or prestige generated from this commuter bedroom suburb of London SW19. It is simply Wimbledon, the home of *the Championships*.

I know Max Robertson and I know Wimbledon. The two are an unbeatable combination. I heartily recommend this book and wish it the greatest success.

FRED PERRY
PO Box 668
Pompano Beach
Florida 33060
USA

AUTHOR'S PREFACE

Writing this book has been a new experience and it leaves me with only one real regret – that, when one is telling the story of a hundred years, one year gets very little space. So much that was worth recording has had to go, so many of the very fine players who did not reach the final stages (or whose talents lay in doubles) do not even get a mention in this despatch. I hope they or their shades will understand.

Apart from the introductory chapter the book is a narrative in chronological form. At the end, as well as the results of all Finals, I have put together some appendices, which I hope will be of use to readers who enjoy either instant or esoteric information.

Many people have helped in the writing of this book. Time was short and worthwhile allies at a premium, so that I was doubly lucky in the ones I found and who gave so freely. Mavis David gave me several hours to tell me stories of her beloved Herman – many of which will be found in the opening chapter. Rex Sterry talked to me at length about the old days and that determined Champion, Charlotte Sterry, his mother. Duncan Macaulay, Wimbledon's far-seeing and efficient post-war Secretary and pre-war assistant in the Referee's office, confirmed much that I had been told and added knowledge and story new to me.

Brian Burnett, the Chairman and David Mills, the present Secretary, told me the sort of stories that are manna to a chronicler. David, his assistant, Chris Gorringe, and Enid Stopke, who runs the office, were helpful far beyond any bounds of professional duty in verifying facts and answering questions. Tony Cooper, Curator of the new Museum, which has been so brilliantly conceived and carried out by Robin Wade, kindly allowed me to use the jacket illustrations of two Museum pieces, and also saved me hours by providing copies of many of the earlier results sheets.

Alan Little, the Museum's honorary librarian, was a constant and most generous source of reference and checking, both personally and by allowing me to borrow his own early records of the Championships. Arthur Cole let me ransack his Le-Roye Productions Limited library to look for illustrations that were different. That we did find some was due to his, Susie's and Mike's wholehearted and sporting co-operation. Buzzer Hadingham and John Barrett of Slazengers' and Ken Weatherly of John Beddington & Partners have all given me amusing and illustrative stories.

To all these I owe a considerable debt. To Fred Perry, who has written such a heartwarming foreword, I can only say, 'Fred, you have made me feel very proud – though I doubt I deserve a tenth of it.' Fred and I have indeed worked closely during many Wimbledons (not difficult in a commentary box) and his deep knowledge of the game, its performers and their tactics, together with our other experts' comments, has been the warp and weft of the fabric of our broadcasts.

Another former star of the court, who now twinkles in the commentary box, is Christine Truman Janes. Chris not only gave me valuable assessments of her leading contemporaries but took time off from her very busy life to read the post-war chapters and pass them for content.

My debt to earlier writers is profound. Personal experience only takes me a third of the way back in the Championships' history. But here I have been so lucky that I could refer to facts established by such contemporaries of the older Wimbledon scene as that eminent *Daily Telegraph* correspondent, A. Wallis Myers (*Leaders of Lawn Tennis*, Amateur Sports Publishing Co. Ltd and *Fifty Years of Wimbledon, The Field*, 1926); that most respected of referees, F.R. Burrow (*The Centre Court and Others*, Eyre & Spottiswoode, 1937); and another *Daily Telegraph* man, John Olliff, fine player and evocative writer (*The Romance of Wimbledon*, Hutchinson & Co.).

Other invaluable reference sources have been Duncan Macaulay's and Jackie Smyth's *Behind the Scenes at Wimbledon* (Collins, 1965) and the latter's *Lawn Tennis* (Batsford, 1953); for the description of the Lambert Chambers/ Lenglen Challenge Round *The LTA Book of the Game* (Max Parrish, 1957); *The Encyclopedia of Tennis* (Allen & Unwin, 1974); E. C. Potter's *Kings of the Court* (Charles Scribner's Sons, 1936): Norman Cutler's *Inside Tennis* (Evans Brothers Ltd); Fred Perry's *My Story* (Hutchinson's); *The Field*, whose editor kindly made me free of its fascinating archives; and unfailingly The B.P. and Commercial Union *World of Tennis* edited by John Barrett. To all these goes my unstinted thanks.

Debt, too, to Judith Morden, my secretary, who typed the fair copy; to Liza, my wife, who subordinated the wants of her own publishers to those of mine; whose editor, Simon Dally, did his best to accommodate my never-ending demands for more pictures; and to Peter Knight of London Express, whose guile and Beaujolais Nouveau persuaded me to have a go.

My deepest thanks go to Dennis Hart, without whose help and guidance as a professional writer, without whose patience and unflagging good humour, this book would never have been finished within its limits of space and time. To you, Dennis, I shall always be very grateful.

And last but greatest of these acknowledgements is without doubt to Wimbledon itself, to the past Champions (many of whom have been unable to resist the bright lure of another crack – at the *Centenary* title), and to the BBC and my colleagues there who have allowed me to enjoy so far nearly four hundred of the best days of my life – at the Championships.

I

WIMBLEDON IS MAGIC

Once, in the Royal Box, Mavis, wife of Herman David, the then All England Club Chairman, said to her neighbour when watching two players hitting up before a match, 'Oh, I know who I want to win, that one, he looks so nice.' Field-Marshal Lord Montgomery leant forward and rebuked her for a flippant viewpoint. 'This is a battle,' he said, 'and you must watch how each player uses the forces at his command.'

Monty liked to come to Wimbledon. He always arrived at 12.30 and expected to be met by the Referee, Col. W.J. Legg, and escorted round Wimbledon on a tour of inspection. It was no part of the duties of the Referee, who is a very busy man, but to Monty he was the GSOI running the show and it was only right and proper that his senior officer should take an interest.

For anyone in the tennis world – players, spectators, administrators alike – Wimbledon is more than a show, Wimbledon is magic. It is without question the most important title any player can aspire to. In 1913 it was granted the official title of the 'World's Championships on Grass Courts', a title voluntarily relinquished after 1923. It did not matter. Wimbledon still remains the premier championship in the world.

It is this partly by right, as being the earliest, but also because it always has been and still is the best run, and with the best facilities for players and public. Admittedly, things can go wrong. An order for the usual 300,000 lavatory rolls lost a couple of noughts one year. In another, after a long day and an enthralling match, a record crowd gave real meaning to the old cliché 'flushed with victory'. They ran the tanks dry.

The courts are the best grass courts in the world and the Centre Court on opening day is like the proverbial billiards table, smooth with a green, velvety sheen as if the marker has just put the brush over it. Even when turning, twisting and skidding feet have bruised it and Wimbledon sun has tanned it, the Centre Court surface produces a true bounce. There are exceptions but usually these are caused by the ball hitting the actual lines, which from year to year have to be in the same place. So with the constant marking, the lime sediment builds up to produce a hardness that has almost the effect of a metal tape and varies the bound of the ball.

The Centre Court is almost completely resown every year and is used only for the Championships or a Final Round of the Davis Cup (that last happened in 1937, when Britain as holder, but without Perry who had turned pro, were challenged and beaten 4/1 by the United States). The Wightman Cup was also played on it in the even years from 1924 to 1938. There has been one exception when during the 'Open' Tennis controversy an experimental pro tournament, sponsored by the BBC to mark the introduction of colour television was held on the Centre Court in 1967. The outside courts have to be used for ordinary members during the season, so they are not resown but re-turfed from the sides of the court and the sides in turn are replaced by turf grown in a nursery.

During the Championships the Head Groundsman and his staff are hard at it from the end of play till late into the evening, watering, patching, cutting (just a light trim), rolling and next morning re-marking. Some players cut up the court much more than others. Adriano Panatta, the Italian ace, is one whom Jack Yardley, the Head Groundsman, hates to see scuffing the baseline turf up with his service action. Sometimes when things got too much for Edwin Fuller, who ruled as a great groundsman after the last war, he used to retire to the pond in his cottage garden and soothe his feelings by contemplating the goldfish.

The Centre and No. 1 Courts have tent-like covers which can quickly be raised by a well-drilled team of groundsmen, and the thirteen outside courts have covers that can be laid flat on the ground. So it is only prolonged or repeated rain that will dislocate the playing schedules. There is one small tradition that has grown up in the preparation of the Centre Court. On the Saturday before the Championships four lady members play it in with a double. On the Monday after, the Chairman's four plays a double which officially closes the use of the Court.

Nowhere is the player better looked after than at Wimbledon. His entry is given hyper-critical consideration as it is weighed against the claims of the five hundred or so others that want to get in. Direct acceptance will go only to 112 players of most proven past performance and current form. Those next in precedence will be asked to take part in the dreaded Qualifying Competition for sixteen places for men and eight for women left vacant in the draw, and the rest politely told that their record does not justify their entry.

The Qualifying Competition has caused more agony, ecstasy, drama and heartbreak than even the most thrilling Centre Court match. To the qualifier getting into Wimbledon means almost as much as for the accepted player to win the title. There was one occasion on a very wet day when normally play would not have been allowed (the Qualifying tournament has an absolute deadline as the Championships cannot wait) and two players had been struggling for hours. One reached match-point. His opponent, who was spread-eagled on the baseline after diving despairingly to retrieve, put up a short lob. The first, playing safe, waited for the ball to bounce. It hit the ground with a squelch – and stayed there. He never recovered and lost the match.

Once in the draw the overseas player is cosseted. Cars bring him from his hotel or from the Queen's Club if he is practising there. The dressing-rooms have every facility, including trained masseurs and physiotherapists. Duncan Macaulay tells of a request just after the last war by Margaret Osborne-du Pont and Louise Brough for a male masseur, as women were not strong enough to work properly on some muscles. The problem was solved by engaging a blind masseur – another instance of the versatility of Wimbledon's administration.

The players have their own restaurant where they are served with hot meals. On the roof of the restaurant is a marvellous position for viewing play on the outside courts and competitors have their own enclosures in the two show courts. They are given very good warning of when they will be needed for their matches. The press and other media are not allowed in the restaurant or dressing-rooms so the players are able to relax and feel free from unwanted interference.

On court they have experienced umpires and linesmen, ball-boys trained specially for the job, the extras a player needs like iced squash drinks or resin for sweating palms at the umpire's chair, balls of tested size and pressure that since 1955 are changed every nine games and courts prepared to as near perfection as weather will allow. On top of this they are living for the two or three weeks in London, so their wives, husbands and sweethearts can go shopping in Bond Street or visit the many sights and places that they have heard and read about all their lives.

The public is superbly catered for. When the gates are opened at twelve noon and the queues surge in, everything is in the luncheon and tea-bars, on the lawns, in the concourse and aisles and in the stands fresh and clean – as if there had been no crowd of 30,000 there the day before, dropping newspapers and sweet-wrappings, cigarette ends and matchboxes and all the other dross that even a well-behaved crowd leaves behind. This rebirth is the handiwork of a posse of students, who clean up as soon as the courts are empty. They also help in the groundsmen's court-covering drill when it is raining. They are hired through the students' union and they have their own tented camp in the grounds.

The ushers are drawn from the various services and they see to it that queuing is orderly. The WRVS man the information desks. The St John Ambulance is at the ready and how essential it is – especially in a heatwave year like 1976. There are sweet kiosks and soft-seat hirers. There is a mobile Post Office and there are the tea-bars and tea-lawns.

Wimbledon is at once a spectacle and an industry. The 300,000 or so enthusiasts who flock there each year are really getting their money's worth, but it is a two-way bargain. They in turn are giving the appreciation of the world's most knowledgeable tennis audience and are providing the income that enables the Championships still to be organized so beautifully, that keeps the Centre Court and others so pristine in appearance (except for the welcome ivy), that allows the All England Club to remain *the* lawn tennis club in the world and that still provides a sizeable income to the LTA, with which it can further the game at club level in this country.

Wimbledon is always refining and perfecting its operation. During the Championships the Committee is split into sub-committees which each have responsibility for a variety of functions. They are constantly looking for and sifting ideas for improvement. These ideas and suggestions from the public are scrutinized and very often acted upon by the Secretary, who will put any radical change before the Committee. A very important addition to the Wimbledon scene this year has been the Centenary Museum, which will be open all the year round. Finely designed, it reflects faithfully the history of the Championships and the development of the game.

At each Wimbledon there are changes and sometimes changes are changed again – even after only one year – when the particular idea that seemed good has been found wanting. Everything possible is done to dot the 'i' and cross the 't' of perfection. Prime examples of this are the arrangements for the press, TV and radio, which undergo changes almost every year. And to ensure smooth relations there is a Press Sub-Committee that meets daily with press representatives, and a member of this Sub-Committee is always available to arrange the many interviews with players requested by the media. These interviews are held in the special press interview room or TV and broadcasting studios built for the purpose.

And the result is more and more players want to enter, more and more spectators want to come, more and more media representatives come each year and Wimbledon is more and more the hub of the lawn tennis world and the high season of its calendar. All this has happened and continues to happen because the club has always been served by men of practical vision who, while preserving the marvellous tradition that is Wimbledon, have never been frightened of change and development, when the time has been judged ripe for it.

Take fashion, for instance. For many years – right up to World War 1 – women players were fettered by the garments that convention forced upon them. Long skirts, choker necks, long sleeves, petticoats galore and straw hats. No wonder women found it difficult to serve over-arm. But exceptions there were – like Lottie Dod's calf-length skirts and sensible cap in the late eighties and early nineties, May Sutton's short skirt in 1905 (just above the knee), acceptable because she was a girl, Suzanne Lenglen's one-piece knee-length dresses that gave her room for her acrobatic leaps, Lili d'Alvarez's trouser dress and Billy Tapscott's omission of stockings in 1929, Helen Jacobs' short-sleeved shirt and Bermuda shorts in 1932, Alice Marble's T shirt and shorts in 1939 – these were the leaders of change before the Second World War.

Afterwards, largely under the influence of Ted Tinling, dresses became more and more decorative and glamorous. The first lace dress was worn by Maria Weiss of the Argentine in 1950, and the same year saw Pat Ward wearing the first nylon dress. In 1947 and 1948 Joy Gannon and Betty Hilton wore coloured trims and in 1949 came Gussy Moran's lace panties. Then the golden girl, Karol Fageros, in 1959. However, efforts in the sixties to introduce all coloured clothes met with rebuff from the Committee and the rule now is for 'predominantly white throughout', which allows fashion some leeway without handicapping opponents by looking camouflaged, or making a harlequinade of what should be a classic tennis scene.

Mavis David, the then Chairman's wife, tells a story of Maria Bueno's panties. Maria was playing on No. 1 Court and the Club's President, Her Royal Highness Princess Marina, Duchess of Kent, wanted to watch her. She and the Chairman went on ahead while Mavis attended to one or two arrangements in the Royal Box. When Mavis got to the No. 1 Court box she found the Princess and Herman convulsed with laughter. When Maria bent over to receive service Princess Marina exclaimed 'She's wearing purple panties.' 'Oh no, Ma'am,' replied Herman, 'I'm sure they're green.' A half-crown bet was made and suddenly all was revealed. Maria's panties were quartered in purple and green, the All England Club colours, to which Maria had a perfect right, being an automatic member as a Champion.

Once when the Queen was coming to lunch before watching play, her Equerry sent a message saying she had been delayed by a visit from U Thant and would be late. Temporary confusion arose. Play must start at two o'clock but lunch would not be over in time. 'Cut the first course [soup] then,' said Herman. 'But we can't,' said the caterer's representative. 'All the menus show the full lunch.' 'Then withdraw the menus,' ordered Herman with common-sense inspiration. This was done. Nobody seemed to notice the loss of the first course and Her Majesty was in the Royal Box for the start of play at 2 pm.

Another aspect of Herman David's pragmatic and firm approach to a problem was when there was a hint in the air that, because of their opposition to apartheid, the Russians might scratch their players if they happened to be drawn against South Africans. It was at a period when much political capital of this kind was being made. He asked the Russians and their team manager to come and see him and told them quite bluntly, 'If you think you might scratch if drawn against South Africans, I want you to say so and scratch now. If you should do so later I promise you I shall personally see to it that no Russian player is accepted here in future.' The Russians played. It was the sort of language that M. Molotov would have found an interesting Cocktail.

Herman David, who took over from Dr Colin Gregory, was a great Chairman of the Club. Having discovered that he almost invariably voiced their collective thoughts, the Committee backed him all the way. They were right behind him on the issue of Open Tennis, of which Herman was the leading advocate – even as far back as 1935 when, in an article in *Tennis Illustrated and*

Rackets Review, he said, 'Just one subject more, that may have a great effect on future Wimbledons. I believe that open tournaments between professionals and amateurs will definitely come. It may be a good thing. It would certainly clear up a lot of cloudy problems.'

Herman was the ideal man to take up the baton of this issue from Colin Gregory, who had been wholeheartedly carrying it when he suddenly died in 1959. In 1964 the All England Club put forward a motion to the AGM of the LTA, asking permission to stage an Open Wimbledon in 1965. The motion, if passed, would have meant that the LTA was seceding from the ILTF, whose policy was at the time rigidly against such adventures. The motion was lost by 88 votes to 40. Although it failed then the motion was a wedge hammered by the progressives into the sickly trunk of the ILTF. Soon it was splitting and Open Tennis did come about in 1968. It still has its problems but at least there is no Shamateurism and for that the All England Club and Herman David can largely be thanked.

The 'cloudy problems' of amateur tennis recall the problems of wet weather when the patient crowds wait, huddled under their umbrellas, the court-covering crew swing into action and the Referee's office becomes awash with enquiries and the ever-changing pattern of the order of play, as he seeks to nullify the inroads on the playing time left to him.

There was no-one better at juggling with his charts than F.R. Burrow, who ruled for most of the inter-war years. A crossword addict (and one who made them up, too), he had the sort of brain that could compute the permutations and quickly compile the order of play that would ease his way out of the latest predicament. Since the war the leading referees have been Colonel Legg and his son-in-law Captain Mike Gibson.

The weather, of course, affects attendances but not as much as one would imagine – Wimbledon crowds are a hardy lot and once they have set their minds on a particular day and everything is arranged (including perhaps meeting up with friends they see annually at the Championships) they are not easily put off. Year by year the crowds have increased. 1967 was the first year that the fortnight's total topped 300,000 and the record was set in 1975 with 338,591. The record for a single day, 37,290, was set on the first Friday of Wimbledon 1975, 27 June.

The Club and Wimbledon have been served well by many. Dan Maskell has been a mainstay of strength and support in various capacities. Before the war he was coach to the All England Club and to the great Davis Cup teams that won and held the cup and his advice, analysis and ever readiness to play practice games were invaluable to Perry, Austin, Hughes and the other team members. After the war he remained the Club's coach until in 1955 he became the LTA's Training Manager. For a quarter of a century he has delighted millions with his TV commentaries, and done much to enhance the prestige of the Club and the Championships.

No Secretary has done more than Duncan Macaulay to make the Wimbledon machine what it is. In 1948 Major David Mills was appointed as his assistant and, having understudied him for years, he was able to slip smoothly into the saddle in 1963. He immediately introduced (1964) the idea of having the programme on Finals days opened with music by one of the leading Service bands. During the Championships he and Duncan lived on the job in the cottage by the Somerset Road gates. On one first morning the telephone rang at 7.30. David answered, groaning a little, and eventually a foreigner came on. 'Are you the Wimbledon Courts?' he asked. 'Yes,' replied David. 'What time am I appearing?' enquired the voice and gave his name, which was not immediately recognizable. 'Hang on,' said David and started thumbing through the order of play. But nowhere did the name occur.

'You're not on the list,' said David politely. 'Are you sure the Referee has put you on today?'

'Oh yes,' said the voice confidently. 'He told me I was remanded for one week.'

But if Wimbledon has been lucky in the men behind it, it has certainly been fortunate in its Royal patronage. The name of the late President, Princess Marina, will always be remembered with a special affection. Not only was her interest in tennis and her delight in watching these great Championships patent to the crowds, as well as to those near her in the Royal Box, but her sincere concern for people is instanced time and again by those who talk of her.

Mavis David tells how the Princess often asked her to go to the Ladies' Dressing Room and enquire after players who had been injured and shown distress. And once, when a small ball-boy was hit in the eye by a ball, the Princess summoned him to the Royal Box and told him how sorry she was and how brave she thought he had been. Rex Sterry tells, too, of the very genuine letter and telegram he received from Princess Marina on the death of his mother, five times Champion, Chattie Cooper, who was thirty-seven when she won in 1908 as Mrs Sterry – the oldest woman to do so. On Princess Marina's death in 1968 her son, the Duke of Kent, became President, since when he and the Duchess have shown the same warm interest in the Championships.

Herman David's birthday was on 26 June and so invariably fell during Wimbledon. One year, soon after he became Chairman, the Committee decided to give him a party, so they sent a message to him saying that something awful had happened and he must come at once for a plenary session. Full of foreboding and wondering what this terrible event could be, he came into the Committee Room and was promptly almost knocked out by a champagne cork rebounding from the ceiling. Later Princess Marina joined in what became a double celebration, for her first grandchild, the Earl of St Andrews, was born that day.

Herman, too, was always concerned to know what was going on. One day, after the Committee had given rather grudging permission on a trial basis for iced lollies to be sold in the grounds, Herman asked the caterer how they were doing. He replied, 'I regret to say, sir, they're selling magnificently.'

Rex Sterry, as Herman's deputy, was his standard-bearer when it came to making speeches. Rex's wit is very dry – vintage champagne. He, too, has had his mishaps in the Royal Box. One very ticklish job that he has to undertake is requesting ladies with very large hats to be kind enough to remove them. Usually his powers are persuasive enough, but he was utterly routed by one regal lady who made no bones about refusing him.

On another occasion Rex was making polite conversation to an African monarch, who had been given into his care by Foreign Service request. As the King, who had said nothing all afternoon, was rising to leave Rex asked him what his impressions had been, to which the reply came 'Yes, thank you. I have enjoyed myself here at Henley.'

Everybody has their Wimbledon story – some many. And Wimbledon is made up of the sum of these stories and all that lies behind them. The Wimbledon press is acknowledged to be the best in the world. Their facilities are good and they make use of them. In such a big tournament, involving the best players in the world, with a crowd that is cosmopolitan, too, there is always plenty of scope for the feature writers – as well as the straight reporters.

For years BBC radio and television have provided many hours of transmission that cover not only the big show courts but several others too. The BBC's Overseas Service sends out daily reports and commentaries to every part of the world. Each year Wimbledon is like a miniature Olympic Games and gets almost the same media coverage. The name of this London suburb is known worldwide, and worldwide it is the blazing ambition of tennis youngsters perhaps one day to play at Wimbledon.

One of the most enthralling and young-inspiring matches ever seen at Wimbledon, and one which gave the media and the crowds a very happy time, was not during the Championships, but in the 1976 Davis Cup European Zone B Final against Italy. It was played on No. 1 Court and the Italians eventually won 4/1, but not before drama of the highest quality had been enacted on the second day.

Leading 2/0 after the first day's singles, the Italians seemed to have the tie in their pockets when in the doubles Panatta and Bertolucci led the Lloyd brothers, David and John, by two sets to love. David, the elder, largely kept the brothers in the match and they won the third set. The fourth was a set of Homeric proportions.

For one thing there had never been a Wimbledon crowd like this one. Italian partisans were there in their droves and kept up an almost continual chanting of 'Ee-ta-lee-ah, Ee-ta-lee-ah'. For a day and a half there had been plenty for them to chant about and their fervent support had unquestionably raised the morale of their players at vital moments. The British support was to begin with nonplussed and produced no real opposition.

But on the second day, led by a stalwart from Essex who possessed a strident car-horn of indeterminate note, the British crowd fought back. And so did the Lloyd brothers. Battle was really joined, between the players on the one hand and the partisans on the other. It was much more like a World Cup football occasion than a scene at Wimbledon.

That fourth set was a humdinger. The British led 2/0 and 3/1, the Italians 4/3. At 5/4 David Lloyd had a set-point but put a backhand cross-court volley out. He had two more set-points, one of which was brilliantly saved by Panatta's return of serve that arrowed down the line. In a seven-deuce game the Italians only broke for 5-all at their fifth game-point. The Italians now led with their service game and at 9/10, 30–40 on his service John Lloyd saved the match with a backhand cross-court chip and a deadly drop-volley.

At 14/15, 15–40, it was David's turn to be beleaguered, with two match-points to save. The first was lost by Bertolucci whose backhand return of serve was mishit. The second David saved with a terrific service to the forehand. Two more were saved by David, one with a backhand dink and the other with a fierce volley. At this point the Lloyds were playing an inspired game and the cacophony of the crowd was overwhelming.

The Italians were broken and only won two more games. The final score to the Lloyds was 6/8, 3/6, 6/3, 18/16, 6/2 in a match which lasted four hours three minutes, including the sixteen-minute interval. It was the greatest Davis Cup doubles most people could remember and an inspiration to those who saw it.

Each year as Wimbledon ends the Secretary, now David Mills, and his very capable office staff under the delightful Enid Stopke, start the ball rolling gently towards the next. Now it is rolling and gathering speed into its second century. Its present Chairman, Air Chief Marshal Sir Brian Burnett, his Vice-Chairman, Bimby Holt, and his Management Committee will face many new problems in the years to come, but they will be foreseen, met and dealt with just as sagaciously as in the past. For Wimbledon must continue and Wimbledon will continue. As an enthusiastic American visitor said to Brian Burnett in 1975, 'There may not always be an England but by God, sir, there'll always be a Wimbledon.'

Arthur Ashe, superb Wimbledon Champion of that year, echoed this verdict just before the American Championships, when he said, 'One thing is clear to me. Notwithstanding the prize money, Wimbledon is bigger than Forest Hills, or anywhere. It is in a class by itself like the world series or your cricketing tests.'

To one man, Pancho Contreras of Mexico, Wimbledon meant so much that he named his son after it. Somewhere there is a Wimbledon Contreras. Perhaps it was enough to turn him to hai-lai (the South American name for pelota).

And now, as the various services and organizations gather and combine to weave the threads of Wimbledon's readiness together, suddenly another year is round, and the magic carpet of Wimbledon is rolled out again. We are transported to delight. It is two o'clock on the first Monday and the Centre Court is already nearly full. The Champion is opening the programme. 'Are you ready?' the umpire asks the players. They should be. Wimbledon certainly is – it has been getting ready for the past fifty weeks.

2

THE BEGINNINGS AND THE BROTHERS 1877–96

On 9 June 1877 readers of *The Field*, an English publication which covered sporting and recreational pursuits, were greeted with this announcement:

> 'The All England Croquet and Lawn Tennis Club, Wimbledon, propose to hold a lawn tennis meeting open to all amateurs, on Monday July 9th and following days. Entrance fee £1.1.od. Two prizes will be given – one gold champion prize to the winner, one silver to the second player.'

This simple statement heralded the world's first lawn tennis championship.

Subsequently *The Field* told its readers that it would be putting up a silver challenge cup worth twenty-five guineas. The prizes and the publicity caused interest, but it cannot be said that the sporting world was taken by storm. The announcement was not a mass appeal aimed at attracting a big gate. *The Field*'s sphere of influence and circulation was among Britain's middle and upper classes. These had already established sporting priorities. One of these was cricket and indeed the playing schedule for that first Wimbledon Championship contained a two-day break on the first Friday and Saturday, to avoid a clash with the Eton–Harrow cricket match at Lord's. In the event, rain on the following Monday caused the postponement of the Final until the Thursday.

Some two hundred spectators made their way by carriage, bicycle and by the new railway to the then outer London suburb of Wimbledon to watch Mr Spencer Gore and Mr W.C. Marshall, the survivors of the original entry of twenty-two, face each other across the net to do battle for the first Wimbledon title.

The scene was recognizable as a tennis tournament as we know it today, but the differences were as marked as the similarities. The rackets were heavy and snow-shoe shaped, players served round-arm and the net itself, five feet high at each wing, dipped to a height of three feet three inches in the middle. These differences were directly inherited from the ancient game of court tennis (Real Tennis), from which the infant game of lawn tennis had recently been derived.

It was this net shape which gave Spencer Gore his opportunity. He saw that with the net rising to five feet on either side, passing shots would not only be difficult but virtually out of the question. So he decided that by getting to the net he could dominate the rallies, in the manner of today's exponent of the big serve–volley game, but of course in those days there was no big serve.

Spencer Gore, an Old Harrovian, was a skilled rackets player – indeed none of the original entry of twenty-two were lawn tennis players – he was quick on his feet and had supple yet strong wrists. So he decided that, instead of playing a gentle baseline game, the main object being merely to keep the ball in play, he would go for the kill. This he did with volleys which were not smashes but which deftly directed the ball wide of his opponent. He did this alternately to the forehand and the backhand, giving the poor fellow such a run-around that one of them subsequently remarked he 'was ready to drop'.

Gore had come to win and he had won – in the Final handsomely, 6/1, 6/2, 6/4. The first All England Lawn Tennis Championship had been staged, the first name inscribed on the roll of honour.

The game, hitherto exclusively a leisurely pastime for leisured classes, had been, unknowingly, launched on the road which was to lead it to becoming a multi-national, multi-million 'industry', followed by millions and creating its own superstars.

The causes of this initial launching lay deep in the character of Victorian Britain. The births of the game and of the first Championships were essentially products of their time.

Britain had a growing middle class. This middle class had energy, energy which developed the industrial revolution, which set up Britain as a colonial power. Some of this dynamism was channelled into the development – and export – of sport. Cricket and football had been well established. These, like indoor rackets and Real Tennis, were more for the skilled and/or enthusiastic exponent. What was still needed was a game which could be played casually, without particularly elaborate facilities.

So, on the spacious lawns behind those solid 'Forsyte' homes, forms of out-door tennis and rackets were evolved, which provided something just a little more physically stimulating than croquet. Like croquet, tennis offered the chance for a young gentleman to converse and mix socially with young ladies. Tennis had the added prospect of the sight of a long skirt, momentarily uplifted, revealing an ankle. But in many circles lawn tennis or 'lawners' was looked down on as 'cissy' and referred to contemptuously as 'pat-ball'.

The All England Club had been founded in 1868 (at a meeting at the office of J.H. Walsh, editor of *The Field*) with grounds at Worple Road, Wimbledon, for playing croquet and holding croquet tournaments. One of its committee members was a certain Henry Jones. Jones was a man of energy and an innovator. He was a keen student of many games and was one of the foremost authorities on whist.

He saw the possibilities in the new game of lawn tennis. In 1875 he persuaded the Committee to set aside part of the ground for a tennis court and also got £25 allocated for equipment. In devoting himself to the cause of developing tennis, Henry Jones did not entirely overlook opportunities for personal reward. When the greater physical exertions of tennis than those of croquet demanded more than the post-game washing of hands, he came to the Committee's rescue (finances being low) by setting up at his own expense a bathroom, all fees for the use of which were to be paid to H. Jones.

With fellow committee members Julian Marshall and C.G. Heathcote he drew up the rules for the first Championship, which he refereed. Those rules have, with minor amendments, governed Wimbledon and world tennis ever since. The scoring terms of real tennis – fifteen, thirty, forty (all minute points on a form of clock scoring) and 'deuce' or 'à deux', i.e. parity (going back to French origins), were retained and a set was won by the first player to get six games.

Before the All England Club produced its rules the emerging game of lawn tennis had in theory adopted a set of rules drawn up by the Marylebone Cricket Club, the controlling body not only of cricket but also of Real Tennis. These embraced at least some of the features introduced by Major Clopton Wingfield, self-styled inventor of Lawn Tennis. Major Wingfield was an incredible character, an entrepreneur in true Victorian style, but who had in his make-up more than a dash of the Elizabethan buccaneer, and even a passing resemblance to the great Sir Francis Drake, a resemblance increased by a favourite garment which was a cross between a waistcoat and an Elizabethan doublet.

Wingfield, a cavalry major, had seen active military and sporting life in the Far East before returning to Britain. He was fascinated by the various racket and ball games beginning to become popular as garden recreation. He saw that this growing popularity had commercial possibilities so he 'invented' the game, calling it Sphairistike or Lawn Tennis, took out a patent and had boxed sets made up comprising equipment and the rules, which he sold. The court was hour-glass shaped, the net being shorter than the baselines.

The rules drawn up by Henry Jones and his colleagues have not only stood the test of time, they had to withstand fierce criticism after that very first Championship. For the net tactics which brought Spencer Gore victory had many declaring that the rules should be changed to counter them.

878 The All England Club, doubtless realizing that continual rule changes would bring confusion and ill repute, yielded by only three inches in lowering the net-posts to 4 ft 9 inches. The club was immediately vindicated in 1878 (34)* through the person of P.F. Hadow, a young planter in Ceylon. He was home on leave in Britain, was introduced to tennis, liked it and played it well (he was a good rackets player) under the tutorage of L.R. Erskine, a friend of the family, who suggested he should enter for Wimbledon.

He won his way through to the All-Comers Final, where he ungratefully beat Erskine, his mentor, in straight sets, so qualifying to meet the much-feared Spencer Gore and his killing net tactics in the Challenge Round (before 1922 the holder did not have to play through). Here, Gore, who had shrewdly

*Up to 1914 figures in brackets indicate the number of players in the draw.

'thought' his way to victory the year before, was himself outschemed. Hadow saw that the counter to the net-rusher was the lob, which he constantly employed to send Gore scurrying back to the baseline.

Hadow's record was truly remarkable. A newcomer to the game, he played through without losing a set – the first of only five men to do so. He beat Gore 7/5, 6/1, 9/7. He then went back to planting and never came to old Wimbledon again. His next appearance was at New Wimbledon to receive his commemorative medal in Jubilee year, 1926.

1879 The Champion of 1879 (45), the Rev. J.T. Hartley, was another who did not allow Wimbledon success to interfere with his calling. He survived the first week of the Championship, and modestly he had not arranged for another preacher to take his place in the pulpit. His parish was in Yorkshire, so he made the then long journey back after his match on the Saturday, took his Sunday service and returned in time for service on court on the Monday. In the All-Comers Final Hartley beat V. St Leger Goold, who was later to be convicted of murder in France and sent to Devil's Island where he died. Hartley 'walked over' in the Challenge Round for Hadow was back in Ceylon.

1880 By 1880 (60) the Championships had become a sporting occasion, stands and new dressing-room accommodation had been built, the entry had increased to sixty, the number of courts to twelve and the price of admission was raised from one shilling to half-a-crown. The vision of Henry Jones was being more than justified. The fortunes of the All England club were transformed. In 1879 the profit for the year was a modest 1s. 10d. which in 1880 shot up to £230 and £760 the following year. This was due entirely to the Championships, which not only contributed most of the money but the success of which drew more and more members to the club.

The crowds were being swelled by the attraction of the personalities now developing. The most notable and the first great lawn tennis player was Willie *1881* Renshaw, who beat the Rev. J.T. Hartley in the Challenge Round of 1881. Willie Renshaw and his twin brother Ernest were not only great players by the standard of their time, but, even with the succession of great players through the years, the name Renshaw keeps a special place in the lawn tennis hall of fame. They matched their own ability by their dedication and application. From their early days they would watch and make notes on the styles of other players. They came from a wealthy family which allowed them to indulge their tennis to the extent of building a court at a hotel in the south of France, on which they could keep up their régime of constant practice in the winter.

They brought to tennis a new concept in doubles play and above all they introduced 'the Renshaw smash'. Unlike the deft Gore flick, this was a fierce overhead volley and it was this which Willie used to counter the lob to win the first of his seven titles, six of them in succession, three of them in finals against brother Ernest (1882 (28), 1883 (23) and 1889 (37)).

1882–3 In 1882 the height of the net-posts was reduced to today's 3 ft 6 inches.

ABOVE The Renshaw twins – a smashing pair.

ABOVE RIGHT Miss Maud Watson – first lady of Lawn Tennis.

RIGHT Lottie Dod – unbeaten at Wimbledon – the compleat games player.

The idea of a service 'let' had been introduced in 1880; previously this had been deemed a good service. In addition players were forbidden to touch the net or volley the ball before it had crossed the net.

In three successive years, 1884–5–6, the beaten Finalist was H.F. Lawford, who had first unsuccessfully challenged in 1880 against Hartley. Lawford was another of the great characters of Victorian tennis, a broadshouldered, up-standing man of firm countenance who, in his shirt with wide horizontal stripes, cavalry-style trousers tucked into socks just below the knee and the whole rig topped with a cap resembling a pith helmet, looked as though he was about to set off to discover the source of the Nile, rather than play tennis. His main asset was his strength and power, which he unleashed in full measure in his forehand drive, like a shell from a cannon.

His clashes with Willie Renshaw contained every thrill for the layman, fascinating contrast in styles for the connoisseur. Their duels were given added spice by reported retorts from both players in the revived controversy about whether volleying should be inhibited by a change in the rules. Declared Lawford: 'It is always possible to pass a volleyer, and I know that when I lose a stroke by being volleyed it is my own fault.' To this Willie responded with, 'Before many years taking the ball off the ground will be quite the exception.'

The principle is still being argued but there was no denying that the nimble, elegant Willie Renshaw had the measure of his powerful, older opponent. In *1884* their first Challenge Round meeting in 1884 (28) Willie took the first six games in eleven minutes and the match in straight sets. This was the signal for Lawford *1885–6* to drive himself harder. The following year he did take a set from Willie and in 1886 (23) after losing the first set to love, by dint of volleying much more he got on level terms at one set all, but Willie won the next two to keep the title. As the Renshaw–Lawford rivalry went on, the box office boomed. In 1885, although the Men's Singles Championship attracted only twenty-three entries, the Challenge Round was watched by 3500 spectators.

1887 The Willie Renshaw–Lawford battles were interrupted in 1887 (16) when Willie had to withdraw from the Championships with the first recorded case of tennis elbow, brought on, it was felt, by his severe use of the newly intro-duced over-arm service. So it was left to Ernest Renshaw to carry the family honour. In the All-Comers Final Ernest ran to a two sets to one lead, but then seemed to become over-cautious and Lawford, ever the relentless battler, powered his way through to the victory which his hard efforts had earned. *1888–9* In 1888 (24) a more determined Ernest Renshaw redeemed the family and gained his revenge over Lawford with a straight sets victory.

The following year (24) the Renshaw monopoly was re-established when Willie, although in failing health, fought his way through the All-Comers Championship for the right to meet Ernest in the Challenge Round. To do so he engaged in an incredible battle for survival in the Final of the All-Comers Singles. His opponent was Harry Barlow who took a 2–0 lead in sets and then

A group of distinguished early
English Players of the late
nineteenth century. *Left to
right:* E. de S.H. Browne; E.
Renshaw; Rev. J.T. Hartley;
Miss Watson; C.W.
Grinstead; Miss Maud
Watson; H.F. Lawford; W.
Renshaw.

Mrs G.W. Hillyard, winner
six times between 1886 and
1900.

went to match-point in the fourth. Even in this dire situation Willie still attacked and got to his favourite net position.

Then, in a hectic rally, he dropped his racket. Barlow, with any shot open to him, played a gentle lob over Renshaw's head. Willie snatched up his racket, raced back to the baseline, retrieved the ball and the point and went on to win the set. Barlow, undaunted, then raced to a five-game lead in the final set, at which point a spectator offered a hundred to one in sovereigns against Willie. He got no takers, and saved himself the hundred sovereigns. For Willie won, surviving altogether six match-points. He went on to beat brother Ernest in the Challenge Round to win his seventh Wimbledon Singles title – a record that has never been equalled in the Men's Championship.

1890
In the 1890 (30) Challenge Round Willie defended against Irishman, Willoughby Hamilton, and gained a 2–1 lead in sets. Hamilton, two years before, had become only the second player to beat Willie at Wimbledon (the first was O. Wodehouse in 1880) and also had wins over both Renshaws to his credit in Dublin. Maybe this gave him a psychological edge, for this thin, pallid Irishman, known as 'the Ghost', fought back against a very weary Willie to win the last two sets 6/1, 6/1. The Renshaw reign was over. Willie was never well enough to compete again. Ernest played in 1891 but lost easily in the All-Comers semi-finals to Wilfred Baddeley and did not try again.

Women 1884–97
By this time male players, for whom an official Doubles Championship was started in 1884 at Wimbledon, were having to compete for the limelight with the ladies. Once again it had been Henry Jones, the great innovator, who had persuaded the committee in 1884 to stage a ladies' championship. There were only thirteen entries. Maud Watson came to the Championships with a record of being unbeaten for two years. She maintained her form to win the first All England Ladies' Singles crown in a close final with her sister Lilian, and she successfully defended against Miss Blanche Bingley the following year (10).

In 1886 (8), attempting a hat-trick, she was again challenged by the persistent Blanche Bingley, whose strength lay in a forehand which would have been an outstanding shot today, but which in the more genteel women's tennis of the day was truly remarkable. She used this weapon to such effect that she won the title. She lost it to the incomparable Lottie Dod in 1887 (5). She consoled herself by marrying (her husband was later to be a great Secretary of the Club as Commander G.W. Hillyard). As Mrs Hillyard she was to win the title five more times and incredibly remain a force in women's tennis until well after the turn of the century.

But first, Wimbledon was to witness the meteoric career of Charlotte Dod. Even allowing for the limited opposition, Lottie Dod merits a special place in Wimbledon history. She did for women's tennis what the Renshaws had done and were still doing for men's tennis. Having initially forged her game by playing with her sister and two brothers, she then modelled it on that of the

Renshaws. A tall tomboy, she brought speed to women's tennis, and with it the smash and attacking net play.

And she did it all by the time she was fifteen. She went on to win five titles in seven Championships and in four of the Challenge Rounds she beat the indefatigable Blanche Hillyard. In 1889 she was on a yachting cruise and did not challenge again until returning triumphantly in 1891 (9). Such was Lottie's supremacy in women's tennis that her first four titles were gained for a total loss of twenty-four games. She never lost at Wimbledon and dropped only one set there. It is said that in her entire tennis career she was beaten only four times.

The Dod meteor burned with fierce brightness. It never died out, but disappeared as suddenly as it had come, when at twenty-one the Champion forsook tennis to devote herself to golf – and become English Champion. She was also a first-class archer and an international hockey player. All in all she had good claim to being called a superstar of sport – perhaps the greatest woman all-rounder the world has known.

During Lottie's absence on the high seas Mrs Hillyard won the title for the second time in 1889 (6) but did not defend in 1890 (4) when the title went to the only Irish girl ever to win, Miss L. Rice, who had to win only two matches. With Lottie Dod off the stage in 1894 (11) Mrs Hillyard won easily but did not play again until 1897 (7), leaving 1895 (9) and 1896 (6) to be won by Charlotte (Chattie) Cooper, later Mrs Sterry and mother of Gwen, a Wimbledon player between the wars, and of Rex, the Club's Vice-Chairman during Herman David's reign. Rex Sterry recalls that at the time of her first win Chattie was staying with her brother, Dr Harry Cooper. She bicycled home to Surbiton and found her brother in the garden pruning roses. 'What have you been doing, Chattie?' he enquired. 'I've just won the Championship,' she replied. Her brother said nothing and went on pruning his roses.

Meanwhile, on to the men's stage, following the departure of the great Renshaws, strode another set of twins, Wilfred and Herbert Baddeley. Their great rival was Joshua Pim, an Irish doctor. Pim's brilliance became a legend. Here was a true artist of the court, whose game was at once powerful and delicate. His art meant more to him than gaining points and victories. He delighted in playing the drop-volley and it was said that he could even deliberately produce a winning net-cord. Here was no percentage player. For Pim the more difficult the situation, the more daring the stroke. He considered a winner should be possible from any position.

Wilfred Baddeley, on the other hand, was a skilful player who knew how to deploy skills to best advantage. With the Champion, Hamilton, not defending, this he did to beat Pim in the 1891 (22) All-Comers Final and conquered him again in the Challenge Round next year (27), but Pim got his revenge in 1893 (27) and held off Baddeley's challenge in 1894 (23) whereupon he retired from top tennis.

Back came Baddeley to regain the crown in 1895 (18) after a tremendous struggle against the Australian W. V. Eaves. Baddeley was at one time within a point of a straight sets defeat. Baddeley lost the title the following year (31 entries, including the Americans, A. E. Foote and W. A. Larned – the latter winning two rounds) to a genial Irishman called Harold Mahony who could attack with volley, smash and even backhand but whose forehand did little more than keep the ball in play. He was a character who came regularly to Wimbledon, taking his defeats and victories in the same carefree way and his eventual success in a fluctuating five-setter was a popular one.

But at that time there were not so many Wimbledon spectators with whom to be popular. After the stirring Renshaw–Lawford battles the tennis of their successors, while being of fine technique, did not have the spectator appeal of their predecessors. And unlike cricket and football which through grass roots participation had already established themselves firmly as popular spectator sports, tennis – once its novelty had worn off – lived by the quality of the show it presented. The evidence of this decline in public interest was revealed in the 1895 loss of £33 on the Championship, a serious matter in those days. In desperation croquet was reintroduced and the extra subscriptions proved a life-saver. The tide was further turning. Three other saviours were at hand, the Doherty brothers and Archdale Palmer, a most astute businessman who became Secretary in 1899.

3

THE DOS AND
OTHER DOERS 1897–1914

Reggie and Laurie Doherty, 'Big Do' and 'Little Do', could have stepped straight from the pages of Victorian schoolboy fiction. They exemplified the current ideals of heroism, they played superbly, showed grace and sportsman-ship on court and modesty off it. Lawn tennis owes them a huge debt. They not only rescued Wimbledon when interest was flagging critically, but helped to stimulate interest in tennis throughout the world.

They were supreme stylists who played just about every shot in the book – by the book which their play was writing. They were fast about the court, but their strokes hardly ever seemed hurried. They were to dominate Wimbledon for a decade and the crowds were to come flocking to see the contrast in styles, as players with varying individual techniques came to try and wrest the title first from Reggie, who won and held the crown for four years, and then from Laurie, Champion for five years. In addition, for eight of those years the brothers combined to hold the Doubles title, engaging in many fascinating battles and holding off many fierce challenges.

There were in fact three Doherty brothers. The eldest, the Rev William Vernon Doherty, was good enough to captain Oxford University, but although a good player, he did not pursue tennis seriously. However, he made an historic contribution to the game by stimulating the interest of his two younger brothers.

R.F. (Reggie), the older by three years, known as 'Big Do' and H.L. (Laurie) as 'Little Do', were both natural sportsmen. At Westminster School both were good at cricket and football. Reggie played in the Wimbledon Singles of 1894 and 1895, the year the brothers first appeared as a pair. They came as undergraduates who had swept all before them at Cambridge, and they took C.F. Simon and W.G. Bailey to a hard five-setter before going out in the first round. Reggie had played in the 1894 Covered Court Championship. He can be said to have reached the Final. But the fact was that due to the dwindled interest in tennis the Singles Championship attracted only two entries. Reggie lost the one and only match to E.G. Meers, an established player, but had done enough to earn mention in *The Field* as 'a young player of great promise whose lawn tennis future will be watched with interest. He has capital ground strokes, volleys hard and clean, serves a capital length and keeps a cool head.'

Reggie and Laurie both entered for the 1896 Wimbledon Singles Champion-ship. Reggie took Mahoney, the eventual winner, to five sets in their first-round match while Laurie extended C.H.L. Cazalet to four sets. He then reached the Final of the All England Plate, instituted that year as an event for early round losers, where he went down only 7/5 in the final set to A.W. Gore, the man who, six years later, was to interrupt the Dohertys' unbroken run of singles successes.

1897   The Doherty reign began in 1897 (31). And what a beginning! Reggie progressed regally, disposing of reigning Champion H.S. Mahoney and Wilfred Baddeley, the previous Champion, and W.V. Eaves who for the third successive year had reached the Final of the All-Comers Singles – all without losing a set. Reggie Doherty, over six feet tall and with finely cut features under dark wavy hair would, in a later age, have had teenagers swooning – as it was he brought colour to many a Victorian lady's cheek. But, suffering from dyspepsia, he endured indifferent health. Most affected were his speed and his stamina.

1898   The following year (37) Mahoney made a determined bid to regain his title. But, having reached the All-Comers Final, he had there to get past Laurie Doherty in order to get a second crack at Reggie. Laurie, tenacious as ever, seemed even more determined that no-one should get past him. Three times in the fifth set Mahoney, leading 5/4 in games, was at match-point. Each time Laurie denied him. This gruelling set was to go to twenty-six games before Laurie earned the right to meet his brother in the Challenge Round, where he pulled back from being two sets down to square 2/2 before Reggie established his superiority in the final set.

In 1898 the reviving interest brought about by the Dohertys' fluent and comprehensive game produced a profit of £70 on the Lawn Tennis Championships. The next year, through the good offices of Palmer, this had leapt to £200 and even the Croquet Championships made £19. A new pavilion was built for £1200 and the Club was restyled The All England Lawn Tennis and Croquet Club.

1899   With Laurie Doherty unable to take part in the 1899 (37) Wimbledon through illness, Reggie was the lone Doherty standard-bearer. But he was not at top fitness nor top form and found himself two sets down in the Challenge Round to A.W. Gore. Gore, playing in his tenth Wimbledon, looked what he was – a successful hard-working Victorian businessman. For him tennis was only a relaxation. But he was a man who played hard as well as worked hard. He was strong, fit and fast. He played from the baseline, happy to engage in long exhausting rallies. His main attacking weapon was his fierce forehand drive. He was so quick on his feet that he was often able to run round the ball and get in a forehand on what should have been a backhand shot. It was such tactics which brought him to the two-set lead against Reggie Doherty. 'Big Do' showed the same coolness which had impressed as a youngster. Refusing to become rattled, he concentrated on accurately placing down the line, so that Gore was forced to play off the backhand which Reggie invariably met

ABOVE R.F. Doherty – 'Big Do' – a master of the game shows perfect backhand counterpoise. His brother, H.L. – 'Little Do' – has been compared with Tilden as the greatest player the game has known.

ABOVE RIGHT Malcolm D. Whitman, American Champion 1898–1900 and No. 1 singles player in the first Davis Cup tie 1900.

RIGHT The American May Sutton, first overseas winner of a Wimbledon title, Champion 1905 and 1907.

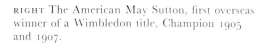

on the volley. So Reggie won two sets to square the match and then took the decider.

An experiment was introduced this year with an unofficial Ladies Doubles, which was won by Mrs Hillyard and Miss B. Steedman. This ran till 1907 but the Championship Doubles only began in 1913, as did the Mixed Doubles.

1900 Reggie's Challenger next year (34) was one of the most remarkable players tennis has ever seen, Sidney Smith, who in the same year became the first All England Men's Badminton Champion. A leg disability prevented Smith from being very mobile. To compensate for this he developed a flat, bludgeoning forehand of such power that it gained the name of the Smith Punch, while in the manner of prize-fighters of the era, the player himself was linked with his hometown to become known as 'Smith of Stroud'.

Smith won the first set of the Challenge Round against Reggie Doherty, but the Champion again got the measure of his baseliner opponent to take the next three sets. The likely prospect of this match of contrasting styles, and a by no means wholly predictable outcome, kept interest high and the crowds flocking. The match also showed that for the title-holder not to be required to play through the tournament, but to appear only in the Challenge Round, had its disadvantages. Playing through the All-Comers Singles could be tiring, but it could also serve to put the Challenger into high gear against a Champion who might be a bit sluggish, especially at the start.

1901 The year 1901 (36) saw a Wimbledon drama to match any of the stage melodramas of the time. Reggie Doherty was in such poor health that his doctor forbade him to play. Indications were that Reggie would take this advice. These arose from Reggie's belief that Laurie would win the All-Comers Singles and that, if he himself scratched, the title would remain in the family.

But after winning the first two sets of his third round match, Little Do was beaten by George Hillyard, the future Club secretary, then better known as a county cricketer who had taken tennis seriously only after his marriage to Blanche Bingley, who between 1886 and 1900 won the Ladies' title six times. Hillyard then met the redoubtable Gore and reached match-point in the fourth set. Gore saved this with a net-cord, going on to beat H. Roper Barrett and C.P. Dixon to win the All-Comers Singles and so earn the right to challenge Reggie Doherty.

So Big Do had to decide. Should he face Gore in the Challenge Round or should he withdraw? Against the advice of his doctor and the pleading of his mother, Reggie decided to play. If the title were to leave Doherty hands, the passing should not be by default. He took the court against Gore, won the first set and went to a 5/2 lead in the second. But he was having to overcome the handicap of his own ebbing strength and Gore's relentless baseline returns. The Challenger took five games in a row to square the match at one set all and, pressing home the initiative he had gained, went on to win the next two sets and the match.

The 'Wizard', Norman Brookes, father of Australian tennis. His fighting spirit is here exemplified by his very shortened grip. He always had his rackets loosely strung for greater control.

'Chattie' Cooper (Mrs Sterry), winner five times between 1895 and 1908.

Big Do had finally been beaten. But the Dohertys were not prepared to bow out of Wimbledon or bow down to a successor. Laurie was now ready to assert his game. Hitherto, he had played well at Wimbledon but with chequered results. Maybe, subconsciously even, he did not want to challenge a brother over whom he had a physical edge. The two brothers never wanted to meet in serious competition, though they enjoyed playing hard-fought friendlies against each other, but Reggie would retire if the pace began to have ill effects on him.

The name of Doherty was not to be kept from the Championship rolls that year. In the Doubles the two brothers held on to their title in a match which marked yet another Wimbledon landmark, for their Challenge Round opponents were the American pair, Dwight Davis and Holcombe Ward. The previous year Dwight Davis had donated the trophy which was to bear his name and he had helped America to win it. Now the Americans were turning ambitious eyes on Wimbledon.

They came to Britain as men of mystery. The crowds were initially intrigued by their black shoes. Players were more concerned with the 'secret weapon' which the Americans brought – the top-spin service which could cause the ball to swerve and break. At the outset the Dos found difficulty in coping with the American spin tactics. One thing that surprised spectators was the way Little Do would try to play back every service, including the faults. The reason was to become apparent. Even as that first set ended Laurie was playing the American service with much greater confidence, and the Dohertys won the next three sets, although the fourth went to sixteen games.

There were those who had had misgivings about the coming of the Americans, feeling that the peaceful family calm of Wimbledon would be broken. But as A. Wallis Myers records: 'By their sportsmanship as by their play the Americans had caught the favour of the crowd.'

1902   The Dohertys came back to defend their title again in 1902. In those Championships Reggie did not enter the Singles (42) but Laurie did. He showed a new authority in taking the title back from the player who had ended his brother's reign. Little Do beat Gore in four sets, the final one to love. But in the Doubles (20) the Dohertys lost their title to Sydney Smith (usually unlucky to be in their shadow) and Frank Riseley, whose one up, one back formation flourished on Smith's famed forehand and Riseley's power and speed at the net. For the next four years these same doubles pairs were to fight out the Challenge Round. In the first three, the Dohertys were winners but in 1906 (28) Smith and Riseley came out on top at the end of a gruelling and stirring five-set struggle.

1903–4   Little Do meanwhile was nobly bearing the mantle he had gained by right of conquest. In 1903 (42) and in the following year (62) he beat Riseley in the Challenge Round. Riseley's path to the Challenge Round was marked by a unique incident. As in 1903 Smith and Riseley met in the fifth round. The first time, after a battle which went to five sets, Riseley won 7/5, 6/3, 7/9, 1/6,

ABOVE RIGHT The durable Arthur Wentworth Gore. He competed at every Wimbledon bar one from 1888 to 1927 and won three times.

ABOVE W.A. Larned, American Champion 1901–2 and 1907–11. He played at Wimbledon in 1896 and 1905.

RIGHT The New Zealander A.F. Wilding, Champion 1910–13.

9/7. In 1904 (62) fifty fiercely fought games saw them at two sets all and at the start of a fifth set. The two contestants, who were again doubles partners, settled for tossing up to decide the winner, rather than subjecting themselves to more punishment.

1905   In 1905 the American Davis Cup team came over to try to wrest the Cup back from the British Isles. In the Championships at Wimbledon their progress and styles of play were keenly watched and analysed. W.J. Clothier was only just beaten in the fourth round by Tony Wilding, who got home 10/8 in the final set; while in the same round Beals Wright, who played in the Davis Cup doubles, took A.W. Gore to four sets. So the leading home players were able to contain this invasion, and at the same time they learned much from the Americans, particularly in the variety of their spin services. This experience was put to very good use at Wimbledon in the Davis Cup tie when the British made a clean sweep.

By now new names were beginning to appear in the lists of entries. Along with the Americans other overseas entries included A. Wilding of New Zealand and the Belgians P. de Borman and W. Lenaire. Also entered for 1905 Wimbledon was N.E. Brookes (Australia). Norman Brookes was to become the Grand Old Man of Australian tennis and give the game a lifetime of service. The 1905 (71) crowds were anxious to see how this early exponent of the serve–volley game would fare against the home players. Brookes provided the answer by getting through to the Final of the All-Comers Singles and just emerged victorious over baseliner Smith.

Brookes thus became the first winner of the Renshaw Cup, donated by the Renshaw family in honour of the great brothers, to be awarded to the winner of the All-Comers event. Following the abolition of the Challenge Round in 1922, the holder thereafter having to play through from the first round, the Renshaw Cup has been awarded to the Singles winner. So it was to be Brookes versus Laurie Doherty in the Challenge Round. Brookes attacked with serve and with volley. 'Little Do' countered with his all-court game, using the lob to turn his opponent's menacing advance into scampering retreat – and to win the match 8/6, 6/2, 6/4.

1906   The next year (69 entries) saw an all-domestic Challenge Round, with Laurie again seeing off the persistent advances of Riseley. But in the Doubles this last year of the Doherty era ended in defeat. Smith and Riseley combined to put on a show of remorseless power, which in the fifth set eventually broke the brave but failing strength of Reggie Doherty, still immaculate in his court manners but physically strained and distressed, a gallant warrior to the last.

It was perhaps fitting that the Doherty Wimbledon reign should end with a mixture of victory and defeat. For as well as the standards of play and sportsmanship they set, they revived the Club's fortunes by establishing new heights of competitive interest. The Dohertys were superlative at the all-court game, but were not so crushingly invincible that they ruled out speculation on whether the various challengers who came up against them would succeed. So, more and more, tennis became talked about and more and more it became watched.

And more and more players came to challenge from overseas. A pair of English brothers had been the centre of the lawn tennis world. Now from the Southern Hemisphere came two men who between them were to share most of the honours until the First World War. Australia had been quick to follow the British lawn tennis lead. The Victorian Championships were held in Melbourne in 1880 and those of New South Wales in Sydney in 1884.

But as in Britain – even more perhaps – it had been purely a social game for the most part and it was not until Norman Brookes, with his devastating volleying game, first hit the headlines in the Old Country that tennis really began to be taken seriously in Australia. Brookes was fortunate to find an ally in Tony Wilding, a brilliant player from New Zealand, and, having wisely formed the Australasian Lawn Tennis Association in 1904, these two were able to team up for Davis Cup matches.

The partnership was of two contrasting characters and styles. Wilding's father, who had emigrated to New Zealand in the 'seventies, had been a good all-round sportsman at home in England. Tony and his brothers and sisters had every chance to grow up in the same way, for there was no shortage of facilities at the Wilding home. He might well have preferred cricket and football to tennis, which so many regarded as cissy. However, a schoolfellow whom Tony disliked heartily, was good at tennis so young Wilding decided to beat him. This he did after six weeks' practice and he realized he could become a champion if he were determined enough.

Going up to Cambridge, he was soon persuaded that tennis offered a greater scope to him than did cricket. He entered Wimbledon in 1904 and in the second round gave the old Champion, Mahoney, a very good fight, though he realized that his strokes could be improved, especially his backhand, for which he did not change his grip. For another thing, he realized that a baseline driving game must be backed by the ability to volley. His top-spin forehand was fierce, and deceptive, though somewhat uncontrolled. With the help and advice of those backhand experts, Mahoney and Reggie Doherty, he improved noticeably and in 1905 was chosen for the Davis Cup team. He had a good eye and strong wrist, as is illustrated in this story told by Wallis Myers. 'He once challenged a friend to a match, agreeing to use only a cricket bat – and very nearly won.' This is strongly reminiscent of Don Bradman practising batting with a cricket stump.

Well-built and possessing perfect health, he still took no chances, training hard for any important match and being careful afterwards to change quickly, before sweat could grow cold and a chill be caught. This dedication to condition went with the desire for fresh air and he loved sleeping in the open. Careful as Wilding was about his own condition, he was careless about dress and other people's possessions, which he often borrowed. Despite this rather cavalier attitude, he was a welcome guest anywhere.

Norman Brookes was totally different from Wilding. The most obvious difference was that he was left-handed. And he was self-reliant and self-taught, smaller of physique but as tough as they come both in body and in temperament. He was a fantastic competitor at any ball game. He had very nearly succeeded at his first attempt in 1905 when he won through to the Challenge Round, having beaten Riseley, Gore and S.H. Smith.

Laurie Doherty held him at bay there. At bay is right because Brookes loved to attack. He had a variety of services, some of them super googlies, all with apparently the same action, and his volleying was adroit and incisive. He soon earned the nickname 'the Wizard'. His brilliant footwork helped what seemed to be an uncanny anticipation. Laurie Doherty had been watching his play round by round and it was only because he studied the Wizard's tricks so closely that he found the answer just in time. Brookes was not abashed. He came off court feeling that next time he would beat Laurie easily.

But next time never came, for in Laurie's final year at Wimbledon, 1906 (69), *1907* Brookes did not play. On the Wizard's return in 1907 (85) he won through the All-Comers, beating A.W. Gore easily in the Final, but by this time Laurie Doherty, the holder, had retired. Indeed, it was largely due to the retirement of Big and Little Do that Australasia, for whom Brookes and Wilding played all five rubbers, were able to challenge the British Isles successfully in the 1907 Davis Cup at Wimbledon. Australasia held this famous Cup for four more years before in 1912 losing once more to the British Isles, who next year ceded to the United States, from which Australasia, spearheaded again by Brookes and Wilding, won it back just as the First World War broke out.

In Brookes's first year as Champion, although he was fortunate in the absence of the four leading home players, the Dohertys, Smith and Riseley, who had all retired, there was still plenty of opposition. In the second round he met Tony Wilding, in one of his many stirring encounters with his Davis Cup partner, and beat him only 3/2. Danger was still there in the form of Karl Behr of America who, after being two sets down, squared the match but faded in the fifth set.

1908   1908 (70) saw the amazing persistence, courage and stamina of Arthur Wentworth Gore rewarded again. He first entered the Championships in 1888 and won the All-Comers Singles only after eleven years, there of course to be repulsed by Reggie Doherty. He gained his first title against a weakened Reggie two years later. His second was won at the age of forty, twenty years after his first attempt. He won, despite his weakness on the backhand. In the Final he beat Roper Barrett in five sets and was perhaps lucky that Barrett had beaten Wilding in the quarter-finals. With Brookes not defending in the Challenge Round, Gore automatically became Champion.

1909   1909 (85) was to be remembered for two things. They were the abominable weather, which for the first time caused the Championships to go into the third week, and the defiant defence of his title by Gore. From a field which included many new faces, and had lost the seasoning of the old Champions, and also Brookes and Wilding, M.J.G. Ritchie came through to beat Roper Barrett in the All-Comers in four sets.

Ritchie was an ambassador for lawn tennis. He had spent many years playing the game, much of it abroad, and he had left a trail of inspiration across Europe. His game was known for its all-round steadiness, deploying a variety of strokes without great power. His defence was excellent and he loved the lob. It was this particular shot which had played a significant part in Ritchie and Wilding's win over Gore and Roper Barrett in the 1908 Doubles Final. Though largely defensive he was no slouch, for, adapting his game to a bit more speed of drive, he had twice beaten Laurie Doherty.

In the 1909 Challenge Round Ritchie is said to have been at his best. The steady qualities of the Challenger, and the long baseline rallies which ensued, provoked many a mistake in Gore's famous forehand, which began to break down. Ritchie led 8/6, 6/1 and then 2/0. At about this point there occurred an interesting incident, which is best told in the words of F.R. Burrow:

> 'I was taking a line in this match, and early in the third set I gave a decision, which was probably wrong, against Gore. Ritchie evidently thought it was wrong. Anyway, he "threw" the next point; and from that moment he was never really on top again. Perhaps it worried him; anyway he played a very different game in the last three sets from that which he had produced in the first two.'

Gore, sensing that his opponent had relaxed, for whatever reason, seized his chance, won the next six games for the set and the last two sets 6/2, 6/2. At forty-one Gore was the oldest champion there had been – a record that has not since been beaten.

1910 (92) had a strong foreign entry, including Beals Wright (USA), R.B. Powell (Canada), Otto Froitzheim and Otto Kreuzer of Germany, the two Fyzees of India, Max Decugis and his protégé, André Gobert of France, from Australia Stanley Doust, now a regular and a beautiful doubles player, and from Ireland J.C. Parke. To round off the strong overseas entry Tony Wilding was there.

Ritchie, winner of the All-Comers in 1909, was unlucky to meet Wilding in good form in the third round, and he lost in four sets. In the quarter-finals Parke took four sets to beat Beamish, as did A.H. Lowe to beat Doust. Easier wins went to Wilding over Froitzheim, and Wright over Powell, both in straight sets. In the semi-finals Wilding beat Parke 3/0, though Wright dropped a set to Lowe.

In the All-Comers Final Wilding and Wright played the classic encounter of baseliner versus volleyer. Not that Wilding scorned the volley. He realized

the importance of gaining the net, once the ground had been properly prepared. To Wright, however, it was the natural place for him to be. Either
following his rhythmic, left-handed service or a well-controlled chop, which
kept the ball bouncing low, he would take the net and more often than not
command it. This he did in the first two sets which he won 6/2, 6/2.

But Wilding, trained as always to a hair, and never turning one, knew very
well that sooner or later the effort of continual serve–volley (it must be remembered that in those days there were few players who trained to modern
standards) would take its toll, and good judgement of the right moment
could bring the initiative into his grasp.

So it happened. More and more his extended opponent failed to be decisive
and was driven back, whereupon Wilding himself came in and volleyed the
winners, to win a rousing match in five sets. In the Challenge Round Wilding,
now more mature and confident and certainly improved on his 1906 form,
reversed his semi-final defeat by Gore in that year, taking the title from him
now in four sets. This was the start of Wilding's four titles running, a distinguished reign.

1911   In 1911 (104) Dixon beat Decugis in a good semi-final match and Barrett
beat F. G. Lowe. The All-Comers Final was another five-setter, with the winner
Barrett this time coming from two sets to love down, to win the match. The
Challenge Round between Wilding and Barrett was a strange affair. Wilding
began well, as expected, and took the first set 6/4. Towards the end of that set
Barrett changed his tactics and began to play half-court shots with no pace.
Wilding found these hard to attack but they drew him to the net, whereupon
Barrett lobbed him. The ploy succeeded so well that Wilding lost his touch and
played like a man bemused. Leading now two sets to one, Barrett tired
rapidly in the heat of the airless Centre Court. Having won the first game
of the fourth set, he lost the next six for two sets all. His legs would now
scarce bear him and he had to retire.

1912   The entry in 1912 dropped to eighty-one and that great campaigner, Gore,
got through once again to challenge Wilding. He played well right through
the draw, keeping on top of some tough matches and, in the All-Comers Final,
he met a much-improved André Gobert and beat him in four sets. This was
the more remarkable – and the crowd recognised this by the ovation they gave
him – because at the age of forty-four he had beaten a man half his age, who
had just won the tennis Gold Medal at the Stockholm Olympic Games.

In the Challenge Round Wilding, who would have preferred to play through
the All-Comers, had too much youth (and now experience) on his side. Gore,
fighting hard, did well to take the third set. Although this was Gore's final
Challenge Round it was by no means his final appearance. He was still there,
fifteen years later, still admired by the crowds, at the sixth Championship at
New Wimbledon in 1927, by when he had competed in all but one Championship for 36 years. He had lived and played through the eras of the Renshaws,

the Baddeleys, the Dohertys, Brookes and Wilding and the new stars of the Twenties, Tilden and the Four French Musketeers.

913   Wimbledon got its highest pre-war entry in 1913 (116). The Championships were becoming more and more international, with overseas players regularly returning to try again. The exception was the 'Californian Comet', red-headed Maurice McLoughlin, whose tremendous service power first gave rise to the description 'cannonball'. His reputation having gone ahead, his first round match with Roper Barrett, still a force, drew tremendous first-day crowds and the gates had to be closed. The match lived up to its promise, for Roper Barrett had seldom played better and took the fiery American youngster all the way, losing only 6/8 in the final set. After that McLoughlin was irresistible, and anticipation of the Challenge Round meeting between Wilding and McLoughlin was so high that hundreds never got near the Centre Court. Ticket touts had the day of their lives, with stand seats reputedly fetching £10.

Wilding had not wasted his time. He had watched McLoughlin's service closely and, to the surprise of all, stood right in to take it, before its great break and jump took it too wide. Wilding also attacked relentlessly the American's weaker backhand. That first set was a battle and when McLoughlin got to 5/4 40/30 and set-point, he put everything he had into a super-fast service. Wilding not only blocked it but, making pace from pace, hit an outright winner. This was undoubtedly the turning point, for he went on to win the first set 8/6 and now had the initiative.

He won the second 6/3 and led 4/2 in the third. Here McLoughlin came again to lead 5/4. The battle swayed to 9/8 and Wilding had 40/30 matchpoint on his own service. The first was a fault. On the second he overstepped the line a long way and was foot-faulted. Many a player would have had his grip on the match loosened. But undismayed, he won the next two points for the title. The Comet had just failed and was not seen in the Wimbledon firmament again.

14   In the last pre-war Championships (102) the 1907 Champion, left-hander Norman Brookes, entered again after a seven-year absence. He immediately showed himself to be in great form, searing through the opposition, winning seven love sets out of the fifteen needed. The All-Comers Final against the German, Otto Froitzheim, seemed to be going the same way when Brookes won the first two sets 6/2, 6/1, and led 5/3 in the third. Froitzheim would not submit and, fighting furiously, took the set 7/5 and went on to win the fourth 6/4. 'Wimbledon Sensation'. The headlines were already being written. And indeed it very nearly was. Brookes never regained that early ascendancy and the final set was hard fought all the way. Many thought Brookes lucky since he had several net-cords at critical points. But he finally gained the day 8/6.

The Challenge Round was played between two men, each full of confidence. Brookes' came from an innate belief in his own competitive ability. Wilding's, fostered perhaps by two recent easy wins over Brookes on the Riviera, was a false confidence – an unusual complacency puffed further by his friends, all of whom told him that he would surely win. Having recently lost some of the keen edge of his interest in tennis, due to business involvement, Wilding had been most uncharacteristic and had not trained for this match. Perfect fitness was so much the complement to his tennis skill, that its absence may have tipped the issue on a particularly hot day. Brookes won his second title 6/4, 6/4, 7/5. Wimbledon was never to see Wilding again. Within a year he had been killed in France.

Women
1898–1914   The Women's Championship, during its first fifteen years, had been fought out between a few strong players. In 1898 (18) the entry was more than doubled. This was the start of a widening interest. Within three years the entry had almost doubled again until, by 1914, it reached fifty-one, still only half the men's field. Women's tennis had yet to be emancipated.

Chattie Cooper, who lost a set only to Miss Steedman in the third round, won through and took the title with a walk-over, Mrs Hillyard not defending. Mrs Hillyard was back next year (17), beating Miss Tulloch in three sets in the semi-finals and Mrs M. Durlacher 7/5, 6/8, 6/1 in the All Comers Final. Her challenge, though, was completely successful, as she beat Chattie 6/2, 6/3.

1900 (16) brought Chattie Cooper promptly back to the Challenge Round, but she failed to unseat Mrs Hillyard who won 4/6, 6/4, 6/4. It was the last of the Champion's six titles. She had deserved them all. She was a great competitor, whose chief asset was a powerful forehand drive. She sometimes wore gloves to improve her grip and followed through so far that the racket head often hit her left shoulder. Like so many of that era her backhand was poor, but she volleyed well and was quick about the court. Three times when she was holder, Mrs Hillyard did not defend. This was because, like any good Victorian lady, she put her duties as wife and mother first.

The girl who had been her main rival over the last five years, Chattie Cooper, now Mrs Sterry, beat her in 1901 (30). In 1902 (27) Chattie lost he title to Muriel Robb. Their match was stopped by rain at one set all and, uniquely, was replayed from the start the next day.

The name of Miss D.K. Douglass occurs for the first time in the 1902 draw. Dolly Douglass was beaten only in the semi-final by Muriel Robb 6/4, 2/6, 9/7. She had given notice that she was to be one of the great champions who, more renowned as Mrs Lambert Chambers, won the title seven times, the last in 1914. Dolly Douglass had her first two wins in 1903 (28) and 1904 (41). But an American girl was to intervene in her run of success. May Sutton, who in 1905 (45) made her first challenge, became the first overseas winner of any Wimbledon title. Dolly had been suffering from a strained wrist but she got her revenge in 1906 (48). The American again reversed things in 1907 (42).

May Sutton developed her skills early in Pasadena by playing against her

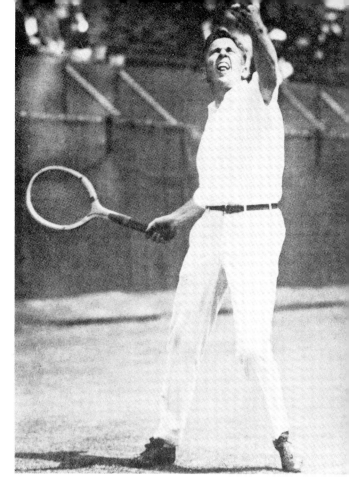

Maurice E. McLoughlin (USA),
American Champion 1912–13 – the
original 'Californian Comet' – delivering
his cannonball.

Mrs Larcombe, winner 1912. Her
husband was Club Secretary 1925–40.

four elder sisters. Once she beat them she was on her way. When she was only sixteen her brother took her to the East Coast where she won the US title at her first attempt. She had a strong forehand and an effective service. She was a good volleyer but did not rely on it. Her main strength was that she had no nerves at all. Being so young, convention allowed her the freedom of shorter skirts which became the envy of the older players who were imprisoned in Edwardian attire. In 1908 (30) May Sutton did not defend and Mrs Sterry won the title without losing a set. Her hardest match was, as might have been expected, in the quarter-finals against Mrs Lambert Chambers, who took her to 6/3, 7/5. That was the last of Chattie Sterry's five titles.

Between now and the war there were only three winners, Dora Boothby in 1909 (37), Mrs Larcombe in 1912 (34) and in 1910 (31), 1911 (34), 1913 (42) and 1914 (51) the winner was Mrs Lambert Chambers, a player whose game had improved considerably since her losses to May Sutton and Chattie Sterry. Her speed and accuracy had increased and her forehand was formidable.

By 1914 Wimbledon had run more than a third of its centenary course. What had started as a game played by the few had developed, but only at the same pace as developments in other spheres of a still slow-moving life. The war was to bring revolutionary change. A hint of the shape of things to come had been provided. In the south of France tennis lovers marvelled at the precocious talent of a fifteen-year-old girl: her name was Suzanne Lenglen.

4

LENGLEN AND TILDEN

Just as the Second World War ushered in a new and exciting – if for some alarming – modern world, so the revival of the All England Championships in 1919 brought in a new era of lawn tennis and with it two superstars of such magnitude that each can lay strong claim to be the greatest player of their sex in the history of the game. Lenglen and Tilden are names which glitter through the record pages of almanacs and encyclopaedias, and the players themselves glittered at the time not only by the prowess of their performance but by the dramatic quality of their glamour. Today we would have called it charisma. Their charisma was all the more remarkable in that it was so immediately achieved, mainly by word of mouth reputation rather than by the instant impact of television.

Suzanne was the first on the scene. Her reputation as a precocious youngster from the Riviera was long known. Many were the stories which flew round about how her martinet coach, Papa Lenglen, had fashioned her accuracy with the light but unrelenting hammer of practice, always practice. He was never satisfied until perfection was reached in any stage, and that was only momentary, for a new mark would be set by placing an object on the far side of the net and telling Suzanne to aim at it repeatedly until she could hit it at will.

Papa soon realized that speed was fifty per cent of a champion's make-up. He made Suzanne skip, sprint and do other training exercises to build up and sharpen her physique. The result of his all-round training was that her perfection of stroke was balanced by her perfection of movement, which was that of a ballerina. This gave her economy, as well as speed, in her court coverage. As a superstar she dressed the part – both on and off court. When Diaghilev introduced shaded silk chiffons, Suzanne brought the fashion to the tennis court by using them for her famous bandeaux.

She made an immediate entrance on a stage which she was to command until her sad exit in 1926. The crowds were so thick round her court at her very first appearance that F.R. Burrow, the new Referee, such a strong personality at the Championships in the inter-war years, was unable to check on a report that she was being illegally coached by her father from the sidelines.

Winning through the All-Comers, Suzanne had arrived at the threshold of her ambition. The clash, which had so long loomed on the wartime tennis horizon, between the reigning and record-breaking seven times Champion, Mrs Lambert Chambers, and the rumoured exceptional player from France, had at last come. Their only previous meeting had no bearing. Mrs Lambert Chambers played Suzanne on the Riviera in 1914 and, although given a surprisingly good game, had managed to win in straight sets.

The Champion's pre-war record had been an outstanding one, and her long jaw and strong face proclaimed her a tenacious fighter. In telling her own story of this match, she said:

'In those days the Champion stood out. I used to practise on the Centre Court every morning, but it is not quite the same thing as playing before the crowded stands, and one knew one's Challenger had become accustomed to the court and the crowd after playing for a fortnight. I was giving Suzanne a good many years [Mrs Lambert Chambers was forty to Suzanne's twenty] and I had not played for five years; many people wondered if it was wise of me to defend my title. I argued to myself that if an English girl came through I would not bother to defend, but if the French girl won the All-Comers event and challenged me, it was up to me to give her a chance to beat the reigning Champion.'

The pre-match tension for both players must have been more than normal before any Final. Apart from the public build-up to it the weather took an unkind hand. The players had changed and were ready when down came the rain. It went on and on and, although the court was covered, the match had to be abandoned for the day. Mrs Lambert goes on:

'The newspapers wondered why I was making such an unnecessary effort as my chance of winning was quite hopeless. I do not think they put me off; on the contrary they rather put my back up and I played the game of my life.'

This is how Mrs Lambert Chambers set the scene:

'In those days, to honour the finalists of the Ladies' Singles at Wimbledon, the Secretary of the All England Club always umpired the match and famous men players were on the lines. I think that this was a gallant gesture and wish it had not been given up. The crowd loved it and cheered the umpire and the linesmen as they took their places. King George V, Queen Mary and Princess Mary were present and received a tremendous ovation on their arrival. Lord Curzon, Admiral Beatty and Mr Hughes the Australian Prime Minister, were some of the notable people I remember being in the Royal Box. There was also the biggest crowd I had ever seen at Wimbledon, many of them having slept out all night.

'It was a perfect day for lawn tennis. There was no wind (wind I dislike intensely) and, although it was hot, the sun was not too intense, there being quite a lot of cloud about. The court as usual was quite perfect.'

So to the match. Suzanne won the first set, in which every point was a battle. Mrs Lambert Chambers, who said she felt on top of the world that day, hit back to win the second. Suzanne, who had shown signs of wilting, now asked for some brandy. Mrs Lambert Chambers tells the story of the final set:

'I must admit I was beginning to feel that I had had enough exercise for one day, and there was another set to be played. After an interval we continued the game. I had become somewhat chilled and I played badly at the beginning of the set. Suzanne quickly went to 4/1 for, as well as my bad lapse, she had some net-cord strokes, which did not help my mood of the moment. However, I tried hard to concentrate and get back my game.

'I then regained my confidence and to my great delight and satisfaction made the score 4 games all. Unfortunately I was getting terribly tired, foot-sore and weary; I had run many miles and, as well as the physical, there was mental tiredness, which perhaps for me was more upsetting. 4-all became 5-all and the crowd was now worked up to a pitch of the tensest excitement. A very long game of terrific rallies followed, which I won to reach 6/5. I then led 40/15 – two points for the game, set and match, and Suzanne in my bag of victories! Alas, it was not to be. That winning point had always been a nightmare to me (whether I was playing the best or merely a rabbit). My arm felt like cottonwool. Also I am afraid that when the umpire called 40/15 I lost my concentration and could not help thinking, "Those newspapers will feel rather small now"; it was a dreadful moment to think like that.'

'Suzanne was evidently also feeling the strain, because she came up to the net on a short return – a thing she would never do normally. I lobbed her but not quite deep enough; she put her racket up and the ball touched the tip of the wood and hit the top of the net, falling on my side! She told me afterwards she never even saw the ball and if ever there was a lucky shot it was that one. Score now 40/30. Suzanne again came up to the net on a short return to my forehand. If I had been asked what I should like her to give me in order for me to make the winning shot – it would have been this one. I had scored over and over again in this match, as in many others, with a short cross-court dipping forehand, which I now played, but unluckily for me (it was, I am sure, because it was match-point) the ball hit the top of the net and fell on my side; why, oh why, could it not have dropped the other side?

'I do not remember anything about the rest of the match but I must have won another game because Suzanne won that set at 9/7 and the match 10/8, 4/6, 9/7.'

(Forty-six games – the longest women's Final until another epic fifty-one years

W.T. Tilden – the Nijinski of tennis, in the view of many the greatest player ever.

Mrs Lambert Chambers – seven times
Champion – in formidable mood.

Suzanne Lenglen (*right*) and Bunny Ryan.
Their doubles partnership won six times
between 1919 and 1925.

later between Margaret Court and Billie Jean King.) The King sent a message to the players asking them to come to the Royal Box as he wished to congratulate them. This proved quite impossible as they were both 'laid out utterly exhausted'. Suzanne's feet were actually bleeding. (Later the King did see Mrs Lambert Chambers and said, 'I don't know how you were feeling but *I* felt quite ill.')

Mrs Lambert Chambers and Suzanne became great friends –

'We frequently stayed together at country house parties and would challenge any men's double – great fun, as we were often the winners. I think perhaps it was a tragedy for her, as for me, that I did not win that first 1919 match, because after that she just could not bear the thought of ever being beaten (which of course is absurd – we have to have our off days). Consequently, her nerves went to pieces and in the end she did not enjoy her tennis at all ...'

But for the moment Suzanne's horizons were boundless. She could do nothing wrong. Her fame spread like a bushfire. The excitement she caused and the arrival of Tilden on the scene next year clinched the argument Commander Hillyard, Secretary of the All England Club, used in persuading his committee that Worple Road could no longer contain the Championships. Accordingly a new ground was found in Church Road – fortunately still Wimbledon – where the venue as we now know it was ready just in time for the 1922 Championships.

In the next seven years Suzanne Lenglen was truly invincible. The only match she failed to win was in the 1921 US Championships, her first and last match at Forest Hills. After losing the first set to the American champion, Molla Mallory, and reaching 2-all in the second, she retired. Unsporting though such an action seemed, there was cause for it. The Atlantic crossing had been terrible, with Suzanne not only seasick for the whole voyage but suffering also from chronic asthma.

She had not come to America to play in the Championships but to raise funds for the devastated regions of France. However, the Americans had entered her for them, with play due to start in two days' time. She was persuaded that it was impossible to withdraw as her entry had caused thousands of advance tickets to be sold. The vice-president of the French Association, M. de Joannis, explained to Suzanne that she must play for the honour of France. Unfortunately, since seeding had not yet been introduced, fate had drawn her against the Champion in the second round. Her first round opponent was asked to withdraw to give Suzanne an extra day's recovery time – but it was not enough.

The only break in her further Wimbledon success came in 1924 when, after an illness in the spring, although winning her first three rounds comfortably enough, she lost a set to Bunny Ryan in the fourth – the second she had

yielded since she first played at Wimbledon. With four days of the Championships left she felt unable to continue in all three events and so scratched from
the Mixed Doubles, thereby getting dispensation from the Referee for a day's
rest. But on the evening of the Thursday, still not feeling fit, she retired
altogether from the tournament.

This was extremely bad luck on Bunny Ryan, who was not only out of the
Singles to a conqueror who then retired but the same lady was also her
doubles partner. That would have meant in the light of historic hindsight
that Bunny's record tally of Wimbledon titles would undoubtedly have stood
not at nineteen but twenty–since she and Suzanne had won the Doubles
for the past five years.

1925 resumed Suzanne's normal sway over both her opponents and the
crowds. But then what promised to be a high-point, even in her career, the
Jubilee year of 1926, turned sour. She arrived at Wimbledon with her mind
unresolved (sic John Olliff) whether to accept a tempting American offer to
turn professional, thereby helping her parents in a difficult financial situation,
or to remain an amateur and continue to enjoy the glamorous life she knew.

These thoughts may well have exercised her as she stood in the opening
day Centre Court line-up to receive her commemorative medal from the
King. But who in the crowd there could possibly have foretold that the ill-
fated 'Lenglen incident' was about to happen – with Suzanne and F.R. Burrow,
the Referee, as the chief protagonists.

All aspects of the famous confrontation have been burrowed into deeply by
tennis historians and it seems to have been a clear case of a strong and
volatile temperament clashing with an authoritarian personality. In the light
of Suzanne's unique standing both as a player and star attraction, a tradition had arisen whereby Suzanne, before leaving the Club at the end of each
day, would be escorted either by Commander Hillyard or a member of the
French team to the Referee's office, to find out what her programme for the
morrow would be. Due to some oversight on the first Tuesday, Ladies' Day,
no-one appeared to escort her. She did not come by herself.

A busy Referee had other things to do besides worry about someone he
was known to regard as a *prima donna*. At the same time, knowing that Queen
Mary was coming next day to watch Mlle Lenglen, it would have seemed
prudent to make certain that she knew her programme, which was to play a
single at two o'clock and a double at 4.30. When she arrived at 3.30 and
was told tersely that she was late, she claimed only to have known about
her doubles and said that she would not play her single first and, if the
Referee insisted upon that, she would scratch from the Championships.

Discussion became hot argument and, reportedly hysteria on Suzanne's
part. So excited did she get that she soon left the ground. The first official
reaction to such an ultimatum by a player would be immediately to scratch
him or her. This was considered, even in the case of the great Suzanne, but

it was felt that the crowd might react badly. Her opponents were unwilling to see her scratched and this face-saver allowed the Referee to postpone her two matches until Thursday and even to put the double on first.

The double was duly played, Suzanne and her partner, Didi Vlasto, lost to the Americans, Bunny Ryan and Mary Browne, after having twice been at match-point. Rain then prevented her playing the single which she won easily next day though, to quote Referee Burrow, 'complaining of pain in her arm and feeling ill'.

On Saturday her only match was a mixed double with Jean Borotra, the last on the Centre Court. When she and her partner came out for the match, some of the crowd appeared to resent the apparent discourtesy to the Queen when she had been kept waiting on Wednesday, and they made clear their displeasure. Borotra, the arch-improviser, responded by doing without a hit-up. He started the match with a grotesque game, in which he sent wild services all over the place, and even into the crowd. Miming his surprise and dismay, he soon had the crowd laughing and they forgot their bad humour. However, it had not gone unnoticed by Suzanne and such a highly strung nature was undoubtedly affected by it. The mantle of idolatry was slipping from her shoulders and she could not bear it.

In the Monday's programme the Referee's wording of 'Mlle Lenglen (if well enough to play) versus Miss C. Beckingham', intended he wrote as 'precaution', may perhaps have been taken by Suzanne as provocation. At any rate, an announcement was eventually made by the Club Secretary, Major Larcombe, that the Champion was retiring from the Singles altogether. Next day a further announcement said she had decided that she was too ill to take any further part in the tournament. She accepted the American professional offer and Wimbledon never saw her again.*

1919   The end of the war – a war which had caused such a violent break in the pattern of life – found the importance of Wimbledon as the peak of the tennis-playing world somewhat surprisingly undiminished, partly due to tradition and the desire on the part of everybody to get back to normal, and partly to the Wimbledon organization which had really become strengthened in the immediate pre-war years to keep pace with the spreading interest – particularly in the men's game.

Widespread interest in the men's game was immediately shown by a record entry of 129 players – 129 because one player from South Africa telephoned the entry of his countrymen but forgot his own. Fortunately for him another entrant withdrew through injury, or the South African could not have been included in the draw. 128 was henceforward the accepted limit with one exception, in 1923 when for some obscure reason 133 appeared in the draw. The women's draw remained an unconstant number until fixed at 96 in 1929. The international element in 1919 was increased by there being demobbed

*She died in Paris on 4 July 1938 and thousands came to line her funeral route.

officers who had not yet gone home and so eight overseas countries were represented. Added to all of which there was the exciting prospect of Lenglen.

The men's event was undistinguished, for few had had opportunities to practise enough to get back to pre-war standards. One exception was Gerald Patterson, a twenty-three-year-old from Melbourne, who was the first Australian with a cannonball service and an all-round more powerful game than his countryman, Brookes, the 1914 title-holder. Algy Kingscote, who had been blooded at Wimbledon just before the war, had three very hard five-set matches against Max Decugis, Pat O'Hara-Wood and C. Garland from the fourth round on – for a total of 148 games.

In the All-Comers Final against Patterson he was very tired and Patterson won easily. In the first ever all-Australian Final (All-Comers or Challenge Round) Brookes, at forty-one, was much slower than the Wizard of pre-war years and the storming young challenger won in straight sets.

If the glamour in 1919 was all Lenglen's, 1920 saw the first challenge of another Tennis Great – William Tatem Tilden. It is curious that the careers of possibly the finest player of either sex should run such parallel courses. The mainsprings in Lenglen and Tilden were utter opposites. Suzanne was wound up by her father. Tilden had an inner coil which made him self-motivated. He won his first tournament as a boy of eight. All his early success came from natural flair and the ability to hit the ball hard. He did not then capitalize on his inborn qualities, playing only by instinct, though at an early date he advocated, 'never give your opponent the shot he likes to play'.

Unfortunately he did not live up to his own maxim, being more concerned with hitting forehand winners and, although very promising, he never seemed to fulfil his potential. Suddenly he realized that there was a 'Why' and a 'How' to tennis and that the mind was as important as the racket arm. Being single-minded he got down to studying the game and analysing it. Soon he had theories and he set about proving them. It was this capacity to think analytically and then perfect, which above all made him the supreme champion he became.

In the 1919 American Championships his opponent in the final was the diminutive Johnston, who had tamed the Californian Comet, McLoughlin, in the 1915 Final. Johnston had used the beautiful symmetry of his game to beat Tilden in three sets. In particular he had assailed Tilden's weak backhand with his own powerful forehand. When the match was over a bystander remarked, 'It took Little Bill to show up that big stiff' – Big Bill Tilden.

The lesson was well taken. Tilden, realizing that he would remain only a finalist and No. 2 to Johnston while his backhand was ill-produced, spent the whole winter working on it, adjusting his grip, grooving it until he had an entirely new stroke. So often when a player does this the manufactured shot does not stand up to the anxieties of competitive play. Tilden had shaped a quality article. And the stroke survived. His game was now pragmatic and fully fashioned. He was ready for the big time.

At Wimbledon Big Bill sailed through his first three matches but then, in his sternest test, Kingscote took him to five sets, clear evidence that only Kingscote's great fatigue had prevented him from giving Patterson a far better match the previous year. In the All-Comers Final Shimizu of Japan, a player of very awkward strokes, led Tilden in each of the three sets, bringing out the best in Big Bill who won 6/4, 6/4, 13/11. In the Challenge Round, Patterson won a probing first set, after which Tilden having discerned a weakness in his opponent's backhand attacked it, and that was the end of the affair.

Tilden's exceptional height and reach gave him his famous cannonball service and added to a commanding presence. By his superb play and magnetic personality, he caught the enthusiasm of the crowd. But, like Nastase in later years, he could blaze with annoyance at inefficient linesmen and lazy ball-boys. The crowd thought these posturings were those of a *prima donna*, and they seemed more so in such a big man. This impatience was a symptom of his own perfectionist nature. He was certainly a sportsman, with a habit of shouting an engaging 'Peach' when an opponent made a good winning stroke.

Tilden, fortified by his Wimbledon win and the knowledge that his hard groundwork over the winter had made him a much more complete player, now started a run of success in the American Championships which was to give him a sequence of six titles, and seven in all before he turned professional. In 1920 he reversed the result of the previous year's Final against Johnston, who was to be his Final victim in five of those six consecutive years. Three of those matches were fantastic five-setters.

1921   In 1921 Tilden won the World Hard Court Championship and soon afterwards fell ill. He was in a London hospital until the second week of Wimbledon. This was the last Challenge Round year. He had four days' light practice but he was still a sick man when he faced Brian Norton, winner of the All-Comers. Norton was a twenty-one-year-old South African with real promise. He also happened to be a firm admirer of Big Bill.

Tilden started quite well but was soon tiring. Norton won the first set 6/4 and the second 6/2. At this point Tilden looked finished. But he always had great courage and he played on. Norton, thinking the match was in the bag, and possibly annoyed by a spectator shouting: 'Play the game, Tilden!' when the Champion used some drop-shots, allowed his opponent to win two sets easily. Tilden then launched himself into a despairing final effort, but Norton got to match-point at 5/4. Tilden's drive seemed to be going out and he was already on his way to the net to congratulate Norton when the ball just touched the sideline. It still presented Norton with a simple winner but, thinking Tilden was ready to volley, he tried a passing shot and failed. Tilden went on to win a match he thought he would not survive.

These last Championships at the old All England Club at Worple Road were both forward and backward looking. Records had been set. There were nearly 170 entries of whom some forty had to be refused. Manuel Alonzo, the Spanish Champion, was the first from his country to reach the All-Comers Final, as was Brian Norton of South Africa. Roper Barrett, born the year Wingfield took out his Sphairistike patent, made this his singles swansong. He was to become the most successful Davis Cup captain Britain ever had. In the early years of the century he had been one of the finest players, who often wove a spell around the best opponents, but lacked the killer instinct. He was at his best in doubles, winning three Wimbledon titles.

The old Club and ground had proved the vision of Henry Jones. It had taken lawn tennis from Victorian pat-ball to become what was already a twentieth-century international sport. It was a fitting moment for the abolition of the Challenge Round. All men would be equal when the stage was taken at New Wimbledon.

5

THE 'FOUR MUSKETEERS'
1922–31

The New Wimbledon was a triumph for tennis architecture and planning. Much was due to the foresight of Commander G.W. Hillyard, the Secretary and former player. The Centre Court, stark new concrete, looked like some vast fortification and it was the showpiece of fifteen courts available to the Referee. It retained the name Centre for old times' sake, though it was to one side, instead of as at Worple Road in the middle of the ground. And the name has always symbolized the highest examination in lawn tennis. No. 1 Court was built alongside it.

Lenglen and Tilden had already been put to the test and signalled their individual supremacy. A new *national* power was now to arise which was to conquer and reach world dominion. France already had her St Joan in Suzanne and now there came four French men who were immediately dubbed the Four Musketeers. Three of them, Borotra, Cochet and Lacoste – all future winners – were making their first appearance. Their various talents and characters so complemented each other that between them, starting in 1924, they won the Wimbledon Singles titles for six years and from 1925 and 1933 they won the Doubles five times. From 1925 when the French Championship was thrown open they won it for the first eight years. Two of them took the American title in 1926 and 1928 and France held the Davis Cup for six years from 1927 to 1932. All these successes were gained by these three men and a partner.

The partner was 'Toto' Brugnon, the only one of the four to play at old Wimbledon. Though a good singles player, he was superb in doubles, the catalyst of any combination he cared to make. His major partners were Borotra and Cochet, with whom he won four Wimbledon titles, five French titles and one Australian. His strokes were not forceful, but they were so well placed that they set up the kill for his partners.

Jean Borotra came from the Basque country where his first love had been pelota, that combination of a scintillating ball game and tumbling acrobatics. Small wonder that his eye and reflexes were hyper fast. Perhaps the rhythm of the pelota swing prevented him from acquiring pure lawn tennis strokes, but his service, his overhead placements and his pugnacious volleys more than made up for this. Moreover, he was utterly determined, schemed cleverly on court and had an electric personality.

His pelota experience also made him the most acrobatic of lawn tennis players the game had yet seen and the most fearless. He would chase the ball anywhere and throw himself at anything if there was a chance of returning it. He was known to end up in the crowd on a lady's lap and then gallantly kiss her hand before resuming the court. He always wore a beret and the crowd adored their 'Bounding Basque'. Borotra was quite aware that these antics did not always endear him to his opponents.

Henri Cochet was small, had a weak service and a very poor backhand, but he was a tennis genius. His game was even more unorthodox than Borotra's. It was built on his uncanny footwork and anticipation, triggered by his speed-of-light reflexes. He engendered despair in opponents, who found winners improvised off their best strokes as Cochet strolled nonchalantly to the net. As with many great players the ball seemed commanded to come to him. A disdainful stroke then dispatched it.

René Lacoste was the last to join this famous band of individuals. Like Tilden he perfected his game by studying his weaknesses, analysing them and eliminating them. For inspiration he watched the best players and learned from them, until he brought himself to a high state of efficiency. Although he lacked the exuberance of Borotra his unassuming and well-drilled game made him a most popular player with Wimbledon crowds.

Whoever coined the expression 'Wimbledon weather' was not thinking of the first Championships at New Wimbledon. They were the wettest on record and fifteen days were needed to complete the meeting, in which there were entries from eighteen countries. The first round was not over until Thursday. If ever the Referee, F.R. Burrow, were called upon to use his crossword-compiling expertise, it was in 1922. However, the dauntless British, headed by their King and Queen, continued to show their increasing interest and support. On three days the gates had to be closed.

For this and the next year the Four French Musketeers were learning and perfecting the drill and tactics which were to make them such a force. Only Brugnon and Cochet got as far as the last sixteen. The title went again to Gerald Patterson, the 1919 winner, who beat his Australian compatriot, James Anderson, one of the biggest hitters the game had seen, in a five-set semi-final, before beating Randolph Lycett easily in the Final. Tilden was not defending and Suzanne Lenglen had said that she had no objection to the abolition of the Challenge Round.

She was nearing the peak of her great career. On the final Saturday, rain having caused postponements, the Referee was in doubt whether to start the Women's Final at such a late hour. Both wanted to play, so rather reluctantly he put the match on. The players went on court at one minute past seven. They were off again well before half past, Suzanne having allowed Molla Mallory only two games.

Leslie Godfree, husband of Kitty McKane and himself a fine player, was alive to his chance when he was the first man to serve on the Centre Court at New Wimbledon. Kingscote having netted his return, Godfree was quick to pounce on the ball and pocket it for a unique souvenir.

1923   If New Wimbledon had been given a wet launching in 1922, the next year made up for it, the sun shining more brightly each day. For 'Little Bill' Johnston 1923 was a lucky year. No Big Bill was there but another American, Frank Hunter, got through to the Final where he gave Johnston no real fight. Little Bill was right on his game that day and with no pressure upon him made a succession of brilliant shots.

In the semi-finals Norton had run him closer, as had Richards in the quarter-finals. At nineteen, Richards was the new boy-wonder and a good volleyer. That Wimbledon was becoming more an entertainment spectacle every year was exemplified by Richards's filmstar entourage. He brought with him a secretary, a typist and a doctor.

In the Women's Championship Suzanne's name was drawn first. It did not really seem significant. She carried on in her royal progress, losing only eleven games in twelve sets. Four of those were in the Final against Britain's young Kitty McKane. And of course she won the Doubles with Bunny Ryan.

This was the year that the French stormed their Centre Court Bastille, and for the first time ever produced the two Finalists, Lacoste and Borotra. It was an extraordinary match which went the full five sets, but each lasted only a quarter of an hour. The average rally was less than four strokes and winners rather than losers abounded. Borotra was shooting all over the court like a jack-in-the-box, which Lacoste the marksman was aiming not to hit but pass by.

The first set was nearly all Borotra, his interception being uncanny. In the second the machine-like game of Lacoste gave him the edge. The Bounding Basque was back with a vengeance and won the third to lead 2–1. For Borotra it was always imperative to win two early sets, whereupon he would coast and reserve himself for a final set assault. Everybody knew this, including Lacoste, and the suspense lay in whether Borotra could last with his uniquely forceful net attack. He volleyed the ball so early that, even if he did not make an outright winner, he often forced errors (or sitters for the next smash) from opponents hustled into uncontrolled strokes. So Lacoste got the fourth set 6/3 and Borotra stormed through in the fifth, 6/4.

The crowd were delighted with Borotra's win and even more so when the two Frenchmen left the court arm-in-arm, both happy that the day's glory belonged to France. Some glory went to veteran Norman Brookes who, in a third round match, showed, like Rosewall after him, that time did little to dim his fire. It was twenty years since his first appearance at Wimbledon. He was playing Frank Hunter, seventeen years his junior, and beat him in five sets. The crowd rose to his courage.

When Suzanne Lenglen retired from the Championships before her semi-final because of the continuing effects of her attack of jaundice, it gave her

Kitty McKane (Mrs Godfree) holds the unique double of winning the Wimbledon title and the All England Badminton Championships, 1924.

The Jubilee Championships 1926: A.W. Gore presented with his commemorative medal by HM Queen Mary. Club Secretary D.R. Larcombe stands behind them while HM the King looks on.

opponent, Britain's Kitty McKane, her supreme chance. Helen Wills, the American girl who was to take over Suzanne's premier position, had quickly settled in at her first Wimbledon and won through to the Final quite easily. Facing her in the Final, Kitty started badly and Helen won the first set 6/4, led 4/1 in the second and had four points for 5/1. Kitty McKane was ever a fighter and desperately she saved those points, starting a run of five games to take the set. Her confidence mounting, she volleyed more and held the initiative to win the final set and the title, 6/4. Kitty McKane had the unique record of *also* being the All England Badminton Champion in 1920–1–2 and 1924.

1925   The Qualifying Competition came into being in 1925. Ever since, to those condemned to earn their Wimbledon right by this tortured route, the Qualifying has seen more drama and felt more anguish than the main Championship ever has. The increased entry which made the Qualifying necessary had been matched by the increase in spectator interest, and the Committee had taken the decision to ration tickets for the first time. The season books were split into two. Later they were split further, into three and now six.

Whereas 1924 had seen a record seven overseas players in the quarter-finals, 1925 provided six – three of them Musketeers. Borotra then had the unhappy job of eliminating a Frenchman, Cochet, whom he beat 5/7, 8/6, 6/4, 6/1. This was a significant win for the Basque, who was normally beaten by Cochet. It was particularly so, since Borotra lost the first set and only just won the long second, in which Cochet was clearly put off by being foot-faulted. His hold on the match was relaxed a little and Borotra seized his chance. Once in charge, he stayed there. René Lacoste, runner-up to the Basque in 1924, beat three national champions on his way to the Final, Washer of Belgium, Jacob of India and Anderson of Australia.

The Centre Court was full to overflowing for this return of the last year's Final. It was quite a different affair. Whereas in 1924 there had been five sets, this was only four but the match lasted much longer. It was Borotra who was out of favour with the foot-fault judge and this seemed to disturb his normally brilliant attacking concentration. Lacoste won the first two sets 6/3, 6/3. The Bounding Basque, denied the early lead he loved to have, refused to submit in three. He had a point for 4/0 and got the set 6/4, going on to 4/1 in the fourth. Lacoste's lead was vanishing and he raised his game again just in time.

This, combined with some near-misses on the volley by Borotra, brought René to 5/4. The bobbing beret led again 6/5 but with his chance there, Borotra sinned with double-faults and the lead was lost. Now with the Bounding Basque's energy – so vital to those net attacks – ebbing, Lacoste ruthlessly applied the *coup de grâce* and won his first title. Normally phlegmatic, he allowed himself a Gallic moment by hurling his white cap high into the air.

The luck of the still seedless draw found the Ladies' Champion, Kitty McKane, in the same half as the great Suzanne who had retired to her before

The lady champions at the Jubilee Championships lined up to receive their commemorative medals. *Left to right:* Maud Watson; Mrs Hillyard; Lottie Dod; Mrs Sterry; Mrs Lambert Chambers; Dora Boothby; Mrs Larcombe, Suzanne Lenglen, Mrs Godfree.

Period peace: Tilden (*left*) and Cochet during the remarkable semi-final of 1927.

the 1924 semi-final. Clearly the French girl thought that there was a score of honour to be settled for she played mercilessly to beat the Champion 6/0, 6/0. Her Final opponent, young Wimbledon débutante Joan Fry, who was the surprise of the Championships, did well to take two games in the first set. Suzanne again won the Doubles with Bunny Ryan and went on to her third triple crown, partnered by Borotra in the Mixed Doubles.

1926   When 'the tumult and the shouting' died and a tearful Suzanne Lenglen had departed the Jubilee Championships of 1926 and Wimbledon for ever, the way was open for lesser mortals. One of these, Kitty McKane (by now Mrs Godfree), had previously seized an unexpected chance when Suzanne withdrew in 1924. Now Kitty did it again in 1926. In the Final she met Spanish champion, Lili d'Alvarez, who, at her first Wimbledon, was another to capture the crowd's admiration for her beauty and her magnetic style.

Lili was an all-out attacking player and used to winning her matches fairly quickly. But Kitty's dogged defence denied this and, having contained her opponent's attack, she counter-attacked and won the first set 6/2. Lili hit back to take the second 6/4 and reached a point for 4/1 in the final set. Taking courage no doubt from the memory of her come-back from a worse position against Helen Wills in the 1924 Final, Mrs Godfree drew on her unfailing resolution and won five games in succession for the match. Her two titles have since been equalled only once by a British girl – Dorothy Round. To add to her Singles title, she and her husband became the first and only married Mixed Doubles Champions.

The opening day of Jubilee year had been a gala occasion. The stage was set, the curtains were about to go up on the King's presentation of commemorative medals to past Champions, when who should make his entrance but the Bounding Basque, who had flown over and changed in the taxi from the airport. He had timed it to perfection.

In an exhibition match Suzanne Lenglen and Bunny Ryan played Kitty Godfree and Mlle K. Bouman. This was to be the last time that the famous partnership of Lenglen and Ryan was seen, for the French LTA had insisted on Suzanne teaming up with Didi Vlasto. The irony was that Suzanne and Didi were beaten by Bunny and Mary Browne, her new partner, in the first round and these two went on to take the title. Nobody was to know that within a few days Suzanne would be turning professional and the Lenglen/Ryan partnership would be dissolved for ever.

The interest of their Majesties, the King and Queen, in Wimbledon was already well established. It had begun through the friendship of Commander Hillyard with the then Prince George, with whom he had served in *Britannia*, and the Prince had first come to Old Wimbledon in 1907. Now, in Jubilee year, the King's son another Prince George, the Duke of York, became the first member of the Royal Family to take part in the Championships. He and his friend and partner, Wing Commander Louis Greig, had entered as reigning RAF champions. His Royal Highness wanted the match played on one of the remoter outside courts, but it was realized that the throng of those who wished to see him would be too great. So the match was played on No. 2 Court.

The RAF champions had drawn a one-time Wimbledon Champion pair, A.W. Gore and Roper Barrett. Duncan Macaulay, later an exceptional secretary to the All England Club, saw this match and says, 'The Duke who was left-handed, was a good player but against such formidable opposition his partner tried to do too much and too often committed the sin of "poaching" rather than intercepting.' Gore and Barrett won in straight sets.

In the Men's Singles French dominance was still there, despite the absence of the holder, René Lacoste, who withdrew for health reasons. Again the quarter-finals had six foreign players in them. Colin Gregory, later the Club's chairman, took Cochet all the way and Charles Kingsley, with his unassuming game, did as well against Brugnon. Borotra beat the great Czech player, Jan Kozeluh, in four sets, while America's Howard Kinsey beat P.D.B. Spence of South Africa. Kinsey was lucky that his semi-final opponent was Brugnon, the least powerful of the French three in singles. Kinsey himself was a defensive player and he and Brugnon had a good fight, Brugnon having five match-points before Kinsey struggled home 9/7 in the final set.

In the other semi-final Borotra, always happiest on the fast Centre Court (or his favourite surface, wood), beat Cochet in a long vacillating match. He was nearly two sets to love down and, had he not stolen the second set from the fire, Cochet must have won. Borotra might have got home sooner, had his approach shots to Cochet's backhand been sounder. In the fourth set he did get them more under control and his volleying then became more effective. He won the fifth set 7/5. In the Final Borotra, playing for France, would have needed a more aggressive opponent than Kinsey to deny him. He mastered the American's defence in a tight first set 8/6 and then romped home 6/1, 6/3.

1927   It was a wet Wimbledon again in 1927 (play going into the third week) but drama was not lacking. At last good sense had prevailed and the leading players were seeded, so avoiding any danger of luck making the draw lopsided, as had happened so often. Because of the weather this was also the first time that play had started at one o'clock. As usual whatever the weather there were record attendances nearly every day.

Lenglen was lost to Wimbledon but Tilden was regained. Since defending his title successfully in 1921 he had been content to compete only at home where he had won every year, until beaten by René Lacoste in 1926. René had just regained his French title and so he had the honour to be seeded No. 1 at Wimbledon. Tilden on his great record had to be 2 while Borotra, the reigning Champion, was 3 with Cochet (4)* and Brugnon (7). What an honour for France – half the seeds – and well it was deserved.

* Figures in brackets indicate players' seeded numbers.

The four top seeds swept to the semi-finals. Borotra beat Lacoste in his own favourite pattern, winning the first two sets 6/4, 6/3. He coasted in the next two, winning one game in each, and bounded through the final set 6/2. The other semi-final between Cochet, who had survived his quarter-final against Frank Hunter after losing the first two sets, and Tilden was to be one of the most talked-about matches ever – posing the eternal question, 'How could a champion of Tilden's mettle and experience allow his supremacy to be usurped when his position seemed to be impregnable?' He was leading 6/2, 6/4, 5/1 and seemed about to realize what he had set out to do – win in three sets, knowing that Cochet thrived on long matches.

Cochet was serving and Tilden, no doubt thinking it worthwhile to go for complete winners since he had two service breaks in hand, put three terrific drives out. 5/2. These three mistakes, tiny as they seemed, were the first breach in the dam through which the flood of Cochet's game was to pour. Tilden lost his service to love! Cochet held his to love. Then came the incredible. Tilden lost his service to love again! 5/5. Cochet's winning sequence of 17 points ran out at 30/0 on his own service, but he took the set 7/5.

The crowd, not believing that this could be anything but a temporary set-back for the American, watched Tilden struggling to regain his rhythm and get back into the match. However, he could not reach the same high level, and was guilty of many double-faults. Cool Cochet went on his nonchalant way as if the result had never been anything but inevitably in his favour – as it turned out to be. The full score was 2/6, 4/6, 7/5, 6/4, 6/3.

In the Final Borotra must have felt that everything was going according to his plan when he took the first two sets 6/4, 6/4. But Cochet the come-back king did it again. True, Borotra took his normal two sets rest (though he still won seven games in them). In the fifth he came bounding back to lead 5/2 and match-point at 5/3 but netted a return of serve. Serving himself at 5/4 he double-faulted on his second match-point. On the third, in a close-volleying rally, Cochet seemed to play a double-hit on the backhand. Borotra claimed this, and had the support of most spectators, but the umpire decided against. The Basque had three more match-points in the same game. Twice he volleyed out and once Cochet brought up chalk on a sideline. Cochet then got to advantage and Borotra again double-faulted. For once Borotra did not have to pretend dismay. Cochet the 'unflippable' won two games for the match.

Helen Wills (1) and Mrs Godfree (2) headed the Women's seeding list. Gwen Sterry, Chattie's daughter, had the honour in the first round of taking the only set which Helen Wills lost. In the semi-finals Helen beat Joan Fry, who in the quarters had put out her fellow 'Babe', Betty Nuthall. Lili d'Alvarez reached the Final for the second successive year but could not stop Helen Wills from winning her first Wimbledon Singles title. This is an understatement. Lili's tremendous attacking game was at its exciting best. Helen more than matched it and the result was a superb display. At the height of the second set battle one rally went to over forty scintillating strokes. Helen won it and, like the losing Boat Race crew, Lili was spent. She won only one more point in the match.

928   1928 had five previous winners in the men's lists, two more than ever before. Tilden (3) was trying again. Once more he was joined by three Frenchmen in the semi-finals, Cochet (1), Boussus and Lacoste (2). This time it was Lacoste who defeated the great American as he had done in the US Championships. In the Final he reversed their recent French title result by beating Cochet.

The Ladies' Final was a repeat of the previous year and Lili d'Alvarez (2) again produced a superlative game to draw the best from a great player. She made Helen Wills run as no-one else had done.

929   An Englishman (Colin Gregory (8)) was seeded for the first time in 1929, when a slight British revival saw Bunny Austin get to the semi-finals and Fred Perry and Dorothy Round make their first appearances. Perry won two rounds. Colin Gregory and Ian Collins (4) reached the Final of the Doubles, where they took the experienced Americans, Allison and Van Ryn, to 4-all in the final set. Collins and Joan Fry got to the Final of the Mixed Doubles and Mrs Watson and Mrs Michell retained their Doubles title.

In the Singles semi-finals, Cochet (1) beat Tilden (3) again, this time in straight sets, and Borotra (2) beat Austin 6/1, 10/8, 5/7, 6/1. Cochet went on to beat Borotra 6/4, 6/3, 6/4. So each of the three great Frenchmen had won the title twice and, unbelievably, the reign of the Musketeers was over.

It was the first Wimbledon Final between the two Helens – Wills (1) and Jacobs (5). Neither had lost a set in getting there and Helen Wills's record was easily sustained without blemish.

30   The rising German star, attractive Cilli Aussem, beat Helen Jacobs (3) in the quarters, only to have to retire at 4/4 in the final set against Bunny Ryan (8) when she fell, sprained an ankle and was carried from the court. So Bunny reached her second Wimbledon Singles Final, where any player it seemed was doomed to be beaten by Helen Wills, now Mrs Moody, who won 6/2, 6/2. In the quarter-finals Bunny had dropped the middle set to Betty Nuthall. Betty fired the public's imagination with her hard-hitting game and this year became the only British girl ever to win the American title.

In the Men's Championship of 1930 Austin, on his fine performance of 1929, was seeded 6 but failed to get to the quarter-finals, though Colin Gregory did – after putting out Fred Perry in a long five-setter. Only Borotra (3) raised the French standard in the semi-finals and Tilden (2) beat him in a typically fluctuating match, 7/5 in the fifth. This was regarded by good judges as the best encounter between them at Wimbledon. Tilden's experience of Borotra's manner of attack enabled him to withstand the storm and take advantage of the lulls, edging ahead when it blew itself out, after Borotra had led 3/1 in the final set.

In the quarter-finals against Allison, Cochet (1) gave himself the usual handi-

THE LAWN TENNIS CHAMPIONSHIPS: THE SEEDED FOR THE SINGLES; AND PLAY.

MRS. F. S. MOODY.
(U.S.A.)

MME. MATHIEU.
(FRANCE.)

FRÄULEIN H. KRAHWINKEL.
(GERMANY.)

MRS. E. O. F. WHITTINGSTALL.
(GREAT BRITAIN.)

MISS H. JACOBS.
(U.S.A.)

MISS B. NUTHALL.
(GREAT BRITAIN.)

MLLE. L. PAYOT.
(SWITZERLAND.)

MISS D. E. ROUND.
(GREAT BRITAIN.)

H. COCHET.
(FRANCE.)

H. E. VINES.
(U.S.A.)

F. X. SHIELDS.
(U.S.A.)

F. J. PERRY.
(GREAT BRITAIN.)

S. B. WOOD.
(U.S.A.)

H. W. AUSTIN.
(GREAT BRITAIN.)

J. BOROTRA.
(FRANCE.)

J. CRAWFORD.
(AUSTRALIA.)

J. BOROTRA, OF FRANCE — HANDICAPPED BY A TOUCH OF INFLUENZA — IN PLAY AGAINST HIS YOUNG COMPATRIOT, A. MERLIN, WHOM HE BEAT: 0–6, 6–1, 6–6, 4, 6–2.

H. W. AUSTIN, OF GREAT BRITAIN, FALLS DURING HIS MATCH WITH M. A. YOUNG, OF GREAT BRITAIN, WHOM HE BEAT: 6–2, 9–7, 6–3.

E. D. ANDREWS, OF NEW ZEALAND, IN PLAY AGAINST J. BRUGNON, OF FRANCE, WHOM HE BEAT: 6–4, 6–3, 6–3.

AS noted under our front page, which shows H. Ellsworth Vines, the U.S.A. champion, in play, the Lawn Tennis Championships were begun on the lawns of the All-England Lawn Tennis Club at Wimbledon on June 20. On this page we present photographs of the seeded men and women players, and also three pictures of the opening stages of play. With regard to these three, it may be said that Borotra faced his first opponent when he was handicapped by influenza, or something unpleasantly like it, and that he had to take a dose of medicine during the match! For all that, he fought hard against his young compatriot, A. Merlin, who played exceedingly well, but could not defeat his more experienced opponent, who won in five sets although he had lost the first to love. H. W. Austin played somewhat slowly and won by his steadiness rather than by his customary brilliance. E. D. Andrews, a former Cambridge player, entered from New Zealand, won a well-deserved victory over Brugnon.

The sixteen seeded players in the Men's and Women's Singles, 1932. Only three failed to reach the quarter-finals. The top insert shows Jean Borotra – 'the bounding Basque' – in full cry.

ABOVE AND BELOW LEFT *Two Musketeers:* Henri Cochet, a player of inspired unorthodoxy. René Lacoste, with his perfected game, the best drilled of the Four Musketeers.

BELOW RIGHT Ellsworth Vines (USA), more famous for his forehand and cannonball serve, Champion 1932.

cap of losing the first two sets but, to the general surprise, the reigning Wimbledon and French champion lost the next set, too. Allison then had a long five-setter with his countryman, Johnny Doeg (4), but in the Final was tamed by his senior citizen Big Bill Tilden 6/3, 9/7, 6/4.

Allison had the consolation of being the first unseeded player to reach a Wimbledon Final. Tilden had at last, after three previous attempts, won at New Wimbledon, gaining his third title at thirty-seven. He was now able as reigning Wimbledon and American champion to end his amateur career on the highest note, and become the first great tournament professional.

1931   Next year, 1931, was no *annus mirabilis*. Helen Moody was not defending and two Germans reached the Final for the first time. Cilli Aussem (1), who had just won the French title, beat Simone Mathieu (3) of France in the semi-finals. Meanwhile, Hilde Krahwinkel (4) just got the better of a grim battle with Helen Jacobs (6) – the conqueror of Betty Nuthall. The Final was a disappointing match for, in a baking fortnight, the courts had become so hard that both girls had blistered feet. Cilli Aussem won in two sets, the only German ever to win a Singles title.

In the Men's Singles, though it was no vintage year, a record was set in the fight for the men's title. The Final between Sidney Wood (7) and Frank Shields (3), both Americans, never took place. In his semi-final with Borotra, Shields fell heavily when leading 4/3 in the fourth set. He managed to finish off the match but, with Davis Cup ties pending, his captain insisted that he should scratch from the Final.

Tilden had turned professional. The Musketeers had shot most of their bolts but great players were waiting in the wings. In the fourth round Fred Perry (5) of Great Britain beat Germany's Gottfried von Cramm.

6

PERRY PREDOMINANT
1932-9

Fred Perry had started his charge but in 1932, before his peak years were reached, a second Californian Comet appeared. H. Ellsworth Vines (2) exploded onto the Wimbledon scene with the most ferocious service and forehand ever seen. Although he dropped a couple of sets in earlier rounds he became better and better as he got the feel of Wimbledon and the Centre Court. His service was getting grooved and the forehand was booming in. In the other half, Wood (5) the Champion went out disappointingly to Satoh, who was stopped by Austin (6) in straight sets. The round before, the quarters, had seen sweet revenge for Austin against Shields (3) for his semi-final defeat the year before.

Perry (4) disappointed his fans when he was beaten in the quarter-finals by Australian, Jack Crawford (8), in four sets. They had hoped to see him play Vines in the semi-final, for the feeling was that he could beat the Californian. Instead, Vines ran through Crawford 6/2, 6/1, 6/3. It was a massacre. Many of his services Crawford could not touch. The same went for many of his service returns.

To reach his first Final Austin had produced his best form, but could have had little hope of winning against the power of Vines. The American hit his big serves and forehands nearly flat, which meant that he had to be right on form to keep them in. Apart from the first set, he was. Vines made enough mistakes to give Austin every chance, had he found his semi-final form. With the first set won 6/4, Vines attained his peak. His service and his forehand were both working to perfection and he blasted Austin out of his way.

The service ace he produced at match-point brought this comment from his victim: 'I did not know which side of me it had gone.'

The historic footnote at this year's Men's title was the defeat of Cochet (1) by Ian Collins in the second round. Quite unperturbed Henri entered for the Plate (the consolation tournament for first and second round losers). He won it, the only former Champion ever to do so.

In any event in which Mrs Moody (1) was competing the result had become a foregone conclusion. In her six matches she lost only thirteen games, beating Kitty Godfree 6/3, 6/0, Dorothy Round (8) 6/0, 6/1, Mary Heeley 6/2, 6/0. At least the hapless Helen Jacobs (5), her Final victim, could rightfully claim that her four games were more than anyone else achieved. To get to the Final she had beaten a string of good names, past and present, Mrs Covell, Mrs Shepherd-Barron, Hilde Krahwinkel, and Madame Mathieu.

Fred Perry and Pat Hughes (3), now the established British Davis Cup pair, who had reached the semi-finals the year before, led Borotra and Brugnon (4) 2–1 in the Men's Doubles Final, and the French pair won the last two sets only by 7/5, 7/5.

1933   Next year, 1933, Perry and Hughes went out to the Japanese Nunoi and Satoh in a five-set quarter-final. Borotra and Brugnon (1) kept their title, though they were taken to four sets by the Australians, Crawford and McGrath, in the quarters and five sets by the South Africans, Farquharson and Kirby, in the semis.

After his devastating form in winning the title at his first attempt, few looked beyond Vines (1) for the winner of the 1933 Singles. But in the second round he dropped a set to a qualifier, A.T. England, and in the quarters lost the third to the huge Czech, Roderic Menzel. In the semi-finals Cochet (3), who appeared more in his old Champion's form than he had in the last two years, lost a close second set to Vines – 6/8 and won the third 6/3. So Vines was in the Final again but his results suggested that he might after all have toes of clay. Crawford (2) was given a tremendous first round match by Maier of Spain who took him the distance. He then had no real trouble before reaching the Final.

The Vines–Crawford Final has always been remembered by those who saw it as one of the best matches ever played on the Centre Court. This was a different Crawford to the previous year. Vines could huff and puff as he would, but Crawford was not going to let his house be blown down. There was no blasting off court this time. There was no ostentation about Crawford's game. He was good, he was accurate and he concentrated. He was of the old school of players. And he looked it, using a square-headed racket and playing with his sleeves rolled down. A positive sign with Crawford that things were getting to a crisis was the occasional rolling up of the sleeve of his racket arm.

Despite the power and reach of the tall Californian he was largely a baseline player, and there was little volleying between these two. It was a mighty battle, the hammer blows of Vines countered by the solid defence of Crawford. Vines won the first set 6/4. Crawford, with the advantage of serving first, led all the way during the crucial stage of the second. He was mainly attacking Vines's weaker backhand, but threw in some tempting high-bouncing balls to his forehand. On some of these Vines made mistakes but he was never fed enough to get his range. At 9/10 down Vines missed out on some of his big serves and Crawford punished the looser ones to break through and win the set.

Crawford's impetus carried him through the third set 6/2. Back came Vines to win the fourth by the same score. Two sets all, twenty-three games each. Crawford, though, in this final set still held the advantage of serving first. At 4/4 Crawford's uncanny instinct told him to come to the net and Vines, now

ABOVE Bunny Austin, finalist to Vines, 1932.
A supreme stylist, who lacked only a severe
service and a complete belief in himself.

ABOVE RIGHT Australian Jack Crawford,
winner of one of Wimbledon's greatest finals
against Vines, 1933, showing the majesty of
his backhand.

RIGHT Perry predominant: his 'table-tennis'
forehand and match temperament won him
the title three years running, 1934–6.

tiring, had not the accuracy to pass him with winners. Crawford won two games, the match and a famous victory.

Vines retained his American title and turned professional. So Wimbledon never saw this great player again. In only two visits he had left his mark, on his opponents, on the crowd and, one is tempted to say, on the court.

Reports that Helen Moody (1) was not playing quite up to her own supreme standards seemed unfounded when she lost only six games in her first three matches. But in the semi-final Hilde Krahwinkel (6) actually took seven games off her. Dorothy Round (2) lost no sets until she met Helen Jacobs (5) in the semi-final. She won 4/6, 6/4, 6/2 to reach her first Final. There was general expectation that she could give the Champion a good game. But to everybody's delight she did much more than that and but for inexperience might have won.

Mrs Moody began confidently and a close first set went to her 6/4. Miss Round then started playing alternately short and long, drawing her opponent in and sending her back. It must have been a new experience to the Champion to be given the run-around. The tactic succeeded and Dorothy Round won the second set 8/6, though a doubtful point went in her favour at a critical moment. This upset both players and jarred the tenor of the last set.

The Champion was tiring and, had Dorothy switched her attack from side to side and kept her on the run, she should have driven home her advantage. Instead she tried drop-shots but they were not good enough to be winners and became losers. Helen Moody, as ever Miss Poker Face, kept her head and won the set and the match 6/3. The title was still hers. The Moody legend remained but the invincibility of it had shown a crack.

1934   Fred Perry gave Britain back her tennis pride. He was remarkable by any yardstick. He was the first Englishman to win the Men's Singles since A.W. Gore in 1909, the year Fred was born, the son of a Labour Member of Parliament. Fred did not start tennis until fourteen – quite late for a future champion. His interest was triggered by chance when on an Eastbourne holiday with his parents he just had to see what was happening on the other side of a wall. The wall happened to be around Devonshire Park, venue for much top-class tennis What he saw excited him and he rushed home to tell his parents that he wanted to play. When windows started being broken some of the Perry neighbours wished that he had not looked over that wall.

Fred's unfettered enthusiasm overcame all obstacles. Hearing that all school-boys could enter for the Queen's Club annual tournament, Fred arrived on the opening morning to enter himself. He so impressed the secretary with his keenness that he was eventually allowed in, although the entry lists had officially closed. At this time, though, Fred lacked the inches he was to grow. Fred had gone to an elementary school and his father intended him to go into business. However, he was so impressed with his son's unremitting efforts to improve his tennis that he decided to give him a year to make good. One of the factors in this decision was the knowledge that Big Bill Tilden had played against his son in a covered courts doubles match at Queen's and had commented that he was a potential World Champion.

Not quite twenty-one Fred was entered for the British Hard Courts Championships in Bournemouth. He got to match-point against Bunny Austin. Fred's friend and mentor, 'Pop' Summers, remarked, 'I felt like throwing my hat in the air for joy when Fred missed that match-point. It was too soon. Had Fred won, the public would have expected him to live up to it. Give him time.'

Fred came to rely on Pop Summers and has never forgotten the wisdom and kindness he distilled. One thing Pop said was 'Fred, you've got to take the ball early.' Fred did, in the manner of table tennis at which he had been World Champion. His famous forehand was directly derived from table tennis, where a wristy flick takes the ball on the rise. Only Fred could do it on a lawn tennis court off the wrong foot and with perfect timing. This early hit ball put the pressure on his opponent. To the tennis purist Fred's strokes left much to be desired. But he did not play to please purists. He played to win, and there was nothing wrong with his ambition and determination. Duncan Macaulay recalls: 'Fred was always certain that he was going to win Wimbledon.'

Both Finalists at 1934 Wimbledon had tough matches on their way there. Crawford (1), the Champion, lost a set each to the talented German, Henner' Henkel, to Britain's Ian Collins, Japan's Yamagishi, America's Stoefen (6) and against Frank Shields (5), who had beaten Austin (4) in five sets in the quarters, Crawford took another five sets. Perry (2) had been 1–2 down against the Czech Menzel in the third round, had beaten Lott (USA) 10/8 in the fourth and had needed five sets in the semi-finals to beat the 1931 Champion, Sidney Wood (7). Fred had an extra incentive to beat Wood, who had ousted him in the 1931 semi-finals. The form of many players had been affected by a mysterious bug called 'Wimbledon Throat'. It had even caused some to withdraw.

Perry was already American and Australian champion but Wimbledon was the one he really wanted. Both started well and Crawford led 3/1. Then Perry went berserk. He reached Arthur Ashe's 'serene high' and stayed there for twelve unforgettable games to lead two sets to love (in the second set Crawford won only eight points) and 1/0. Crawford, temporarily finding the eye of the storm, got back into the match and at one time looked like winning the third set when he served at 5/4. But Perry broke back and held his own for 6/5. Crawford serving reached 40/0. Perry pulled him back to deuce and then got to match-point. Crawford, determined to get to the net before Perry, foot-faulted on his first service. His second went into the net.

Fred Perry had achieved every tennis player's dream ambition. He could wake up and it would still be true. To him it meant more than to most. He had had to do more to get there.

Wimbledon had gone wild at the excitement of a British Champion at last.

Was it possible, with Mrs Moody not defending, that Dorothy Round (2) might succeed in making it a double? Helen Jacobs (1) the American Champion hoped not. She had waited long enough in the wings. She had lost only one set on the way to the Final against Britain's Joan Ingram in the third round. Dorothy lost two, one to Mrs M.R. King in the fourth and one to Madame Mathieu in the semi-finals.

As in the Men's Final but unlike so many finals, both players started well and Dorothy Round, getting the fast pace of the court first, took the lead and kept there to win the set 6/2. It was a swaying battle in the second set. Helen Jacobs led 5/3 but was pulled back. She got to 6/5 and then Dorothy Round had a fit of overhitting and lost the set. She managed to break Helen's service in the first game of the third set. Her length and accuracy then deserted her, so that Helen led 2/1 and had a point for 3/1. Helen Jacobs then hit what looked like a tremendous winner, but Dorothy just got her racket to it and had the bonus of a net-cord, which left her opponent helpless.

It was the sort of incident which changes fortunes. She again broke Helen Jacobs's service in the important seventh game and then, scenting a win, attacked from the net. Three superb volleys gave her 5/3 and she won the next game at her second match-point to take her first title. Britain's Double had been achieved.

Bunny Ryan, that inveterate American competitor at Wimbledon since she arrived in Britain in 1912, won the Doubles with Madame Mathieu (1), making her bag of Wimbledon titles a record nineteen. Her total tally is reputed to have been 659 tournament wins, including the last women's championship of Imperial Russia. The amazing thing is that with her record she never won a major singles title. When she started at Wimbledon corsets were still the order of the day and she recalled them hanging up to dry, bloodstained from the wounds they had inflicted.

1935   To a man like Perry (1), who had a real Champion's make-up, once the goal had been achieved it should and would be done again. He was the Champion. He looked the Champion and he made every opponent feel that he was going to stay the Champion. He dropped a set here and there in 1935, one in the semis to Crawford (3), but there was no sense of danger about it. In the Final he met Gottfried Von Cramm (2). Perry had just won the French title so had now won all four major honours, but not the grand slam in one year. In Paris he had beaten Von Cramm on the slow surface of Roland Garros. He was quite certain he would beat him on the Centre Court, and told Duncan Macaulay before the match, 'I shall beat him 6/2, 6/3, 6/4.' The score was actually 6/2, 6/4, 6/4.

Austin had again reached the last eight by his fluent play, and there had been beaten by a nineteen-year-old American newcomer called Donald Budge, whose backhand alone already gave him the hallmark of greatness. He took a set in the semi-finals from Von Cramm. For Australia Crawford and Quist (2)

Gottfried Von Cramm, unluckiest of finalists 1935–7 against Perry and Budge. Like Austin, a superb stylist.

Dorothy Round, winner 1934 (a happy double with Fred Perry) and 1937.

took the Doubles, and went on to win the American title. Quist was to win again fifteen years later with John Bromwich, and again they went on to win the American. From 1937 to 1950 he won ten consecutive Australian doubles titles, eight of them with Bromwich. Fred Perry won the Mixed Doubles with Dorothy Round (3) and a third British success came with the win in the Womens' Doubles of Freda James and Kay Stammers (3).

This year Mrs Moody had returned for the Ladies' Singles but was seeded at No. 4. Joan Hartigan (8) from Australia was a fine and improving player, who beat the Champion, Dorothy Round (1), in the quarter-finals, so the prospect of another clash between Miss Round and Mrs Moody was unfulfilled. Helen Moody was not match-tight, having played little in the last year. She lost a set in the fourth round to the all-out attack of Miss Cepkova of Czechoslovakia, but beat Madame Mathieu (5) easily enough and overcame Joan Hartigan 6/3, 6/3. Helen Jacobs (3) had an easier draw and made reasonably light weather of reaching the Final. In the semi-finals she beat Hilde Krahwinkel, now Mrs Sperling (2), who had just won the French title. In the quarter-finals the German had been too experienced for Britain's attractive and rising young star, left-handed Kay Stammers, winning 7/5, 7/5.

The Final was by far the best of the four Wimbledon Finals the two Helens had played. There was much at stake. Helen Jacobs had lived in the shadow of Helen Wills Moody since they had grown up together, attending the same college in San Francisco. They had played each other eight times and Helen Moody had won seven of them. The eighth had been in the American Final two years before when, at 0/3 down in the last set, Mrs Moody retired with a back injury, later diagnosed as 'a slight displacement of a vertebra'.

Mrs Moody started the Final in high mettle. Her drives streamed to the lines and she was soon 3/0. Helen Jacobs then won twelve successive points to level at 3/3 and have Helen Moody at 0/40. She clawed back those three points, just salvaged the game and ran out for the set 6/3.

Helen Jacobs's length and passing shots were so good in the second set that, despite serving a double at set-point, she won it 6/3. The third set was tense. Nerves took their toll. Helen Jacobs was the first to recover and went to 4/2 and then 5/2. She had a match-point at 5/4. This she lost, then volleyed out twice. Helen Moody was level. Her calmness and resolution brought her the next two games for the set and match at 7/5. It had been a sustained and courageous fight by both girls, and they were cheered for several minutes. Helen Moody had now equalled the record of Mrs Lambert Chambers – seven times a Wimbledon champion.

1936   Fred Perry (1) joined the immortals in 1936 when he won the Singles title for the third year running, a record never repeated since the Challenge Round was abolished. The consistent Austin (7) again reached the semi-finals, where the German champion, Von Cramm (2), beat him in four sets and Perry lost his only set at the same stage to Budge (5). These scores suggested that Perry

The American rivals: RIGHT
Helen Wills – *'la belle Hélène'*
– holder of the record eight
singles wins at Wimbledon.
BELOW Helen Jacobs, four
times her Final victim, and
1936 winner in her
absence.

was as confident as ever. But an accident during the year before, which had undoubtedly cost him the American title for the third year in succession, had kept him out of tennis for seven months. He had lost to Von Cramm in the French Final and he was not match-tight. He needed reassurance from his friends at the beginning of the fortnight but his results soon re-established his own. By the Final it was the old Perry, certain of winning.

Except for the first game, the Final was a sad anticlimax. That first game lasted nearly eight minutes. There were ten deuces with three break-points to Von Cramm. On each of these Perry served an ace. At the start of the next game Von Cramm pulled a muscle in his right leg. Although in pain, he concealed it so well that it was some time before Perry realized it. Von Cramm insisted on playing on and limped through game after game, Perry winning 6/1, 6/1, 6/0. Perry then helped the British team to win the Davis Cup for the fourth successive year before turning professional.

Mrs Moody did not defend and at last Helen Jacobs (1) had her just reward, winning the Final 6/2, 4/6, 7/5 against Mrs Sperling (5). Although Dorothy Round reached only the quarter-finals, as did Kay Stammers, it was overall a good year for Britain. Freda James and Kay Stammers again won the Doubles and Fred Perry and Dorothy Round the Mixed, and to cap it all, it was an all-British Men's Doubles Final with Pat Hughes and C.R.D. Tuckey (2) beating Charles Hare and F.H.D. Wilde 6/4 in the final set.

1937-8   The years 1937 and 1938 hang well together in Wimbledon history. Donald Budge completed a double triple crown, and Von Cramm as ever played beautifully to reach the Final for the third time. Budge was the third Californian Comet. His immediate success was not as great as Vines's, who won at his first attempt. But he was the first player to complete the grand slam of the four major titles in one year (1938) and he was the major factor in the United States winning the Davis Cup in 1937 and 1938. Budge then turned professional in 1939 and beat both Vines and Perry in his début at Madison Square Garden. In winning his two Wimbledon singles titles he lost only one set.

As well as his pre-eminent backhand he had a good forehand, a tremendous serve and a sure command of his volleys. To this natural display of talent he learned from Perry to add aggression. Here was another superstar.

In the 1937 Final Budge (1) beat Von Cramm (2) who must have felt the unluckiest Wimbledon competitor ever. He was beginning to peak when Fred Perry was at the top and then immediately suffered Budge. In 1939 he would surely have won but was unable to play. He would have been at his best during the war years and was still to show fine form in post-war years. His was the most beautiful game of fluent and poised grace. A match between him and Austin was a feast of stroke-making.

It was Austin who was Budge's (1) Final victim in 1938. Bunny Austin (2) himself was a perpetual near-miss, twice in the Final, three times semi-finalist and four times a quarter-finalist between 1929 and 1938. With Perry he was a

Donald Budge, Champion 1937–8 (when he was the first winner of the grand slam), possessing the most famous backhand of all time.

Centre Court appearance: Two of the most attractive pre-war players: left-handed Kay Stammers (*right*) with Sarah Palfrey Fabyan (USA) in the semi-finals, 1939. Kay won 7/5, 2/6, 6/3.

Alice Marble, winner 1939, who brought a new concept of powerful all-round play to the women's game, an all-time great.

key man in Britain's successful quest for and holding of the Davis Cup 1933-6. All he needed to be a Champion was a more severe service and a killer instinct.

1937 saw Dorothy Round win her second title, losing only one set in the Final to the popular Polish girl 'Jed' Jedrzejowska. Jed, besides being a Finalist, could count another feather in her cap. In the semi-final she beat Alice Marble 8/6, 6/2. To be able to say that in after years was something.

In 1938, the year Budge achieved his grand slam, Helen Moody set up her record eight Wimbledon Singles victories. She did it in her fourth Final against Helen Jacobs, the first woman to reach the Final unseeded. This was a one-sided affair because Helen Jacobs injured an Achilles tendon when practising the day before with Tilden.

Her ankle was bandaged and at 4/5 in the first set, finding the bandage too tight, Helen Jacobs tried to loosen it. As the two players were at the umpire's chair she asked her opponent if she could stop to take it off. Helen Moody did not reply, but concentrating so intensely as she always did, she may well not have heard. The umpire gave his permission and, while it was being done, Helen Moody stood her own ground. However, she was known never to speak to opponents during a match.

She was the most dedicated and single-minded player, the epitome of concentration, often not knowing the score, just playing for every point as if each mattered equally. Everything about her was tightly controlled and appearances were perfect. The effect was cold and when she bowed out it was as if the Snow Queen had gone, still wearing her crown – in her case an eyeshade.

1939   Helen Jacobs had not the strokes of Helen Moody – her forehand was chopped – but she, too, had great dedication. She was back at Wimbledon in 1939 as No. 2 seed but this time could not capitalize on Mrs Moody's absence. Indeed, she was beaten with surprising ease by Kay Stammers (6) in the quarter-finals, 6/2, 6/2, and the British girl went on to beat Sarah Palfrey Fabyan (8) in a match which hinged on the first set which Kay took 7/5.

However, like everybody else who played her, Kay Stammers was no match in the Final for Alice Marble (1), who had already won the American title twice and was to win it twice more before turning professional. Alice Marble brought the men's power game to women's tennis. She was the complete champion and, in this last pre-war Wimbledon, won the triple crown, the Doubles with Sarah Fabyan and the Mixed with Bobby Riggs. Her coach was 'Teach' Tennant, who was later to nurture the game of Maureen Connolly.

The Men's Champion was Bobby Riggs (2), who also won the triple crown at his first Wimbledon appearance. It is significant, though, that Von Cramm (who did not play at Wimbledon) beat Riggs with ease in the London Grass Courts Final at Queen's Club the Saturday before the Championships.

Riggs was a highly confident player with a good all-round game though he played mainly from the baseline. He had the temperament for the big occasion and is said to have made a lot of money from the bookmakers when, after his

Queen's defeat at the hands of Von Cramm, he backed himself heavily to win the Wimbledon title. In the Final he beat his fellow countryman, Elmer Cooke, in five sets.

The curtain fell in 1939 on the Second Act of the Wimbledon drama. This time the interval was to last for seven years.

7

AMERICAN TAKE-OVER
1946–50

1946 Wimbledon emerged from the war slightly bruised – there had been the odd bomb about – but all was very quickly put so nearly to rights that the 1939 fans coming back to their Mecca might well have thought that from a tennis point of view no Second World War had existed.

All this was largely due to the organization for which Wimbledon has ever been justly famous. The Secretary, Lt-Col. Duncan Macaulay, who had been an assistant referee up until 1939, soon got a firm grip on the running of the Championships. Duncan Macaulay put his stamp on Wimbledon and he ran it all by what he called his black book. This was a harvesting of experience set out in one loose-leaf book, to which he constantly referred and added in the light of experience. Self-analysis has long been a characteristic of the All England Club which for fifty weeks a year is a private club, but which devotes ninety per cent of its effort and administration throughout the year to making the Championships the nearest thing to perfection in international sport.

There was evidence of the war in the 1946 programmes, still very much utility efforts with only eight pages and practically no advertisements. A notice on the inside of the back cover and outlined in black, headed 'Bomb Damage to Centre Court' told of the night of Friday 11 October 1940 when a 'stick' of five 500 lb bombs straddled the Club grounds. The first bomb demolished the tool-house. The second bomb of the 'stick' fell on the roof of the Centre Court, the third fell in Church Road at the northeast entrance and the last two produced bunkers in the Wimbledon Park golf course.

The damage to the Centre Court meant a loss of approximately 1200 seats.

After a gap of seven years the known form of the various entrants in many cases scarcely existed, and the Referee must have had an extremely hard job working out acceptances and seeding. However, some of the old guard needed no introduction. Among the men Tony Mottram, who was to serve Britain so well in the Davis Cup, had played as a youngster in 1939, since when the RAF had claimed him with so many others, including John Bromwich of Australia, who had lost their best years and their best chances. Jaroslav Drobny, a name unfamiliar to most people then, but who was to become a Wimbledon heart-throb, had surprised everybody in 1938 with a victory over his famous fellow Czech, Menzel.

But the name on everyone's lips as the seemingly inevitable winner was Jack

ABOVE 1946, the first post-war Final. Yvon Petra (*left*) of France shares his triumph with loser Geoff Brown of Australia.

ABOVE RIGHT Jack Kramer – 'Big Jake' – the player-computer.

The Australian John Bromwich, one of the closest near-misses Wimbledon has known, in typical half-volley pick-up. Like Brookes, his rackets were loosely strung for better control.

Kramer (2) of America. He and his compatriot Tom Brown were also favourites
for the Doubles. Kramer was a tennis machine, superbly built with the big
American serve–volley game and, although seeded No. 2, he was most people's
favourite.

Kramer's fourth round match with Drobny soon had Number 1 Court
bursting at the seams. Kramer took the first set 6/2. The second, a titanic
struggle, eventually went to Drobny 17/15. This battle killed Kramer's hopes.
He had aggravated during earlier matches a blister on his racket hand. This
was further inflamed during the gruelling struggle with Drobny. Drobny took
the third set for a 2–1 lead. Kramer equalized in the fourth. But the effort with
his blister had been too much and, with the crowd by now firmly supporting
Drobny, the Czech won the deciding set.

Drobny went on to beat Pellizza of France in straight sets in his quarter-
final. In the semi-finals he himself was beaten in three by Geoff Brown of
Australia. Brown had previously beaten the graceful Lennart Bergelin (8) of
Sweden 13/11, 11/9, 6/4. Bergelin, like Cochet before him and Krishnan a little
after, was a marvellous player of the unorthodox shot – especially the half-volley
which he would pick up and turn into an attacking stroke as he wandered
seemingly quite casually to the net. Today Bergelin is the man who brought
Bjorn Borg to his pinnacle as Wimbledon Champion and Swedish tennis
therefore has a double debt to him.

Dinny Pails (1) of Australia floated comfortably through the quarter-finals.
There he met Yvon Petra (5), of France, who put out Pails in four sets. Poor
Dinny. On the way to Wimbledon that day he missed a train on the London
underground. What made things worse is that he was playing on the Centre
Court. He finally got on court twenty minutes late. Having kept everybody
waiting, including Queen Mary, he was sweating with nerves and at a
tremendous psychological disadvantage when he faced up to the big serve game
of Yvon Petra.

Petra did not so much play tennis as perform. He was something of a mixture
of Tilden and Nastase. The effect was that of a one-man whirlwind. Nor did
it help Pails that each time he was at the Roller end he could see the familiar
sight of Queen Mary, straight-backed, awe-inspiring in her familiar toque hat.
She was flanked by the Chairman of the All England Club, Sir Louis Greig –
who had partnered her son on his Wimbledon appearance – and Lady Greig,
who took it in turns to hold Her Majesty's sunshade, relieving each other when
an anguished look indicated that the arm was tiring.

After disposing of Pails, Petra beat Tom Brown in five hard-hitting sets.
Came the Final and Petra rushed to a two-set lead against Geoff Brown (3)
and most of those present thought he was on his way to quick victory. Brown
did not think so. There then unfolded a memorable David versus Goliath
battle with Brown conceding at least seven inches to his giant opponent.

Petra used his full height to unleash cannonball serves and thundering

The American invasion, 1946: the finest women's four of all time. *Left to right:* Louise Brough; Margaret Osborne (du Pont); Doris Hart; Pauline Betz. Brough and Osborne won the first of their five titles.

Margaret Osborne in action. She was one of the few women who could play a backhand smash.

forehands. But Geoff Brown, small as he was by comparison, yielded nothing to Petra for power. The wind-up and the arc of his right-handed service swing were short, but the resulting delivery was so fast that he reminded one of a spring, tightly coiled, being suddenly released. And, like David with his sling, Brown served with such accuracy that, despite a low trajectory which allowed little margin of error, he served many aces. He had a left-handed forehand and an explosive two-handed shot on his backhand.

Brown came back at Petra just as furiously as Petra had come at him and he rallied to win the third set. Petra seemed to have got clear again when he made it 5/3 in the fourth set and at 40–15 was serving for the match. Whereupon Brown hit two devastating two-handed returns of service straight through the incoming Frenchman, followed by yet a third which left the crowd – and Petra – stunned. Brown won the game and took the set. Petra hit back in the final set which he won 6/4 for the match and the title.

Petra had many distinctions. To start with he was born in Vietnam, then the French colonial possession Indo-China, learned to play tennis in his bare feet and also became a soccer goalkeeper of some repute. After his family returned to France, Yvon became a barman and spare-time tennis player. During the last war he was badly wounded in the leg and taken prisoner. By one of the ironies of war, when it seemed that the leg would have to be amputated, it was saved by the skills of a German surgeon who operated on prisoner Petra.

The Ladies' Singles in 1946 produced more evidence of the old guard. Names like 'Jed' Jedrzejowska, who had conquered Centre Court hearts as a girl of sixteen, Kay Menzies (4) – Kay Stammers that was – one of the most beautiful stylists who must surely have won during the war years, the Woodgate sisters, Mme Mathieu, that persistent French Champion who was a Wimbledon semi-finalist in the years 1930–2 and again in 1937, Mrs Jean Bostock (6), Mrs Uber (winner of the All England Badminton title in 1935), Mrs Strawson, one of the leading pre-war players, Joan Curry, Mrs Betty Hilton, and Betty Nuthall.

However, the favourites were clearly the Americans who had come with a tremendous reputation which was fully justified when they provided all the semi-finalists. The No. 1 seed was Pauline Betz. She played like a ballerina. Her grace was matched with power and she never had a qualm in taking the title without dropping a set. Her opponent in the Final was Louise Brough (5), who had had a big semi-final battle with her great friend and doubles partner, Margaret Osborne (2) (later du Pont). These two were to dominate the women's game for some years to come in company with Doris Hart (7). What had been hinted at by the masculine effectiveness of Alice Marble's winning game in 1939 was now an established fact. Top American women played like men. They produced big serves and they could volley.

1947   Jack Kramer (1) had come to Wimbledon in 1946 to win. He failed, probably because of his blistered hand (although he himself refused to use that

Pauline Betz, the first post-war Champion. She might have joined the greats but turned professional.

Betty Nuthall, the only British girl to win the American title (1930), playing on No. 2 Court, 1946.

as an excuse). Kramer simply became more determined, if that were possible, when he came back in 1947. For it meant that he was now a year behind schedule. The Kramer plan was that he would win Wimbledon, turn professional and make his living from tennis. He had decided that to make good in the world he would do it through what he was best at – playing tennis. So, from being an excellent player he turned himself through unrelenting practice into a great one.

With his crew-cut hairstyle and lean, keen looks, Jack Kramer appeared to have come straight from the Harvard Business School. That was how he played. He brought to tennis the percentage game. His tennis was intelligent. It was powerful, it was ruthless. His victory in the Final against fellow American, Tom Brown (3), saw him drop a mere six games and throughout the whole Men's Singles tournament he lost only thirty-seven games. He must figure in a list of Greats.

Kramer, majestic and efficient on court, was to prove to be a businessman with the same flair, allied to shrewdness. After winning Wimbledon, which opened the golden door to professionalism as a player, he quickly became a promoter running an international 'circus', signing big cheques as readily as he had served and volleyed, but as ever with great thought behind the flourish.

The limitations of reigning Champion, Yvon Petra (7), were exposed by Tom Brown in the quarter-finals and Brown beat elegant Budge Patty fairly comfortably to reach the Final. In the fourth round Patty had put out John Bromwich (2). Bromwich, like Geoff Brown, double-handed on his right-hand side and left-handed on his forehand, showed just how ambidextrous he was by serving right-handed. He was a marvellous touch player and brilliant at doubles. Like his great compatriot, Norman Brookes, Bromwich used a loosely strung racket that gave him longer 'feel' of the ball. He deserved to win the Singles title, which he would surely have done but for the war. In 1947 we saw for the first time a tall American, all arms and legs which seemed to take time to unfold. His name was Bob Falkenburg (8). We were to see more of him and hear much more about him in 1948.

In the absence of Pauline Betz, who had left the amateur scene, Margaret Osborne (1) took the Women's title with a good win over Doris Hart (3). To get to the Final Doris had beaten Louise Brough (2) in a great three-setter while Margaret Osborne had outgunned the graceful South African, Sheila Summers (7). Many more battles royal were to be fought between these queens of the court.

1948   In 1948 John Bromwich (2) of Australia looked destined to achieve the crown which all who saw him knew he deserved. He was seeded No. 2 to America's Frankie Parker (1), a rather mechanical player who relied more on length and percentage shots than inspiration. Matters seemed set all the more fair for Bromwich when Parker was beaten in the fourth round by the graceful Swede Lennart Bergelin. Bergelin was then blasted out by Bob Falkenburg (7), the gangling American with a cannonball serve, very reminiscent of Vines. Bromwich, with his soft wiles, bringing delicacy to the two-handed stroke, got through to the Final without dropping a set and must have felt in form enough to handle anything that Falkenburg would throw at him. But neither he, nor anybody else, knew what was in store.

Many names were being applied to the lanky Falkenburg – Daddy Longlegs or, when he sank to his knees, the Praying Mantis. Bromwich had set-points for the first set but lost them to his own nerves and fine passing shots by Falkenburg. The American then appeared wantonly to throw away the second to love and was already taking time out lying on the ground or stalling before service. Bromwich's concentration and confidence were disturbed, and his habit of shaking his head from side to side in a slow, rueful manner became even more noticeable. His game disintegrated in the third set which Falkenburg won 6/2. However, more 'throw-aways' by Falkenburg helped Bromwich to square the match at 2-all and the Australian got to 5/3 in the final set. At this point Falkenburg repeatedly held up play, sinking to his knees in Praying Mantis fashion. Clearly these delays took toll of Bromwich's nerves when he was at the brink of his ambition. He led 5/3 and 40/15 on his own service. Falkenburg saved the first match-point and a missed volley cost Bromwich the second. A brave passing shot by Falkenburg saved yet a third. Bromwich was clearly over-anxious and, having missed these chances, he scarcely won another point.

After the match, Fred Perry said to 'Buzzer' Hadingham, now Chairman of Slazengers who always provide the equipment for the Championships, 'Well, I'd say Falkenburg won by thirty-four falls to thirty-one headshakes.' There was much controversy over Falkenburg's 'stalling' tactics. It did emerge subsequently that he suffered from a thyroid deficiency.

Bromwich gained some consolation when, in partnership with Frank Sedgman (3), he won the Doubles title, putting out top seeds Falkenburg and Parker in the semi-finals and winning the Final against Brown and Mulloy (2).

Tony Mottram had the Centre Court crowd roaring for him in his fine third round win over Cucelli of Italy. It was a most exciting and exhausting match, the score being 6/8, 6/3, 10/12, 9/7, 6/2. When at the Roller end, where the Groundsmen's friends have privileged seats on and in front of the roller itself, they heard Cucelli several times say 'Basta! Basta!' meaning 'Enough! Enough!' To English ears it sounded rather different. The roller is the pony roller with long shafts that was brought from Old Wimbledon to prepare the new Centre Court. The stands were built round it before anyone realized that it could never be got out.

There was no question mark against the winner of the Ladies' Singles. The year 1948 saw the inauguration of a conspicuous reign by a tennis queen. After a Final in which points were fluently and fiercely contested, Louise Brough

(2) beat Doris Hart (4) 6/3, 8/6 to win the first of her four singles titles. By her record alone Louise Brough has earned a special place in lawn tennis history. In all she was to win thirteen Wimbledon singles and doubles titles and in the Wightman Cup, playing for America between 1946 and 1957, she was unbeaten in twenty-two rubbers.

Her record is all the more incredible when it is remembered that she thrived among other fine players. That 1948 Wimbledon well illustrates this. No country has ever fielded four players of such quality as Louise, Margaret du Pont (1), Doris Hart and Pat Todd (3), who made up the semi-finals line-up in the Women's Singles. Louise and Margaret then beat Doris and Pat (2) in a memorable Doubles Final 6/3, 3/6, 6/3. The partnership of Louise and Margaret was even greater than their combined singles talents. They were to win the American doubles title an unbelievable twelve times.

1949   Wimbledon 1949 was a vintage year. It provided Drobny's first final; it saw the one appearance in his heyday of one of the all-time greats, Ricardo 'Pancho' Gonzales (2); and the year also marked the only appearance ever in the singles of F.R. 'Ted' Schroeder, the No. 1 seed who quickly became known as 'Lucky' Ted.

A second round match between Van Swol of Holland and Abdessalam of France provided the only occasion on which a squirrel has invaded and left its mark on the Centre Court, helping to change the course of at least a minor piece of tennis history. Van Swol, a big blond Dutchman, was 5/3 down in the final set and seemed to be sinking fast to the little Algerian Robert Abdessalam. Suddenly the Centre Court was engulfed in roars of laughter. A squirrel was sitting pertly in possession of the court. Van Swol, quick to seek any relief, turned his racket head upwards and had a sit-down. A linesman made heroic but unavailing efforts to catch the offender. After an enthralling chase in which the squirrel jinked like a rugby three-quarter it was caught by a ball-boy, who promptly got bitten for his pains.

The squirrel was removed, chattering unrepentantly while the ball-boy received attention from the St John Ambulance men. It was then back to the tennis. Van Swol, who had been able to enjoy a respite of some three minutes, rallied to win the set and the match 13/11.

After his great win over Kramer in 1946, Jaroslav Drobny (6) had become the Wimbledon crowd's 'favourite' favourite. So there was relief when the American champion, Gonzales (2), was removed from Drobny's path by little Geoff Brown of Australia. None of the tennis lovers who later came to idolize Gonzales could know that he would not be seen again at Wimbledon until the arrival of Open Tennis in 1968 – when he was still a giant but no longer a Colossus. It was a further tribute to Gonzales' ability and drawing power that he did not need the glamour of a Wimbledon title to be the No. 1 target for Jack Kramer to sign for his professional circus.

In the semi-finals Drobny beat John Bromwich (5), losing only six games.

Bromwich had previously got some revenge over his Final conqueror of the previous year, Bob Falkenburg (4). It had been another astonishing display. Falkenburg, when leading 2/0, threw twelve games to take a rest and Bromwich won the final set 6/4.

Lucky Ted Schroeder had almost gone out in the first round to unseeded Gardnar Mulloy, who took the first two sets. Schroeder with his chunky appearance and sailor's gait was just like Popeye and he did have a corn-cob pipe. You almost expected him to take a handful of spinach to sustain him through the next crisis. Not that he ever seemed to need sustaining. He was as cool as the refrigerators he sold – even in the tightest of situations. In the quarter-finals, against the speed and power of twenty-one-year-old Frank Sedgman, he found himself trailing two sets to love. He squared the match. In the final set he was called upon to save several match-points. On one of these he was foot-faulted on his first service. His nerve held and he went for a good and not just safe second serve, rushed the net to take the vital point and eventually the set at 9/7. In the semi-final he came from 2–1 behind to beat South African Eric Sturgess (7), who brought all the delights of the pre-war baseline game to his graceful stroke play.

In the Final against Drobny Schroeder dropped the first set, won an inspired second set to love, took the third but lost the fourth. He got to 5/4 in the final set and then clinched the title in the grand manner by serving out the last game to love.

The line-up for the Women's Final was Louise Brough (1) against Margaret du Pont (2). It produced a memorable three-set battle which went to forty-three games. Louise won the first four games and Margaret the next five, and it was not until the third break of service that the set went eventually to Louise at 10/8. Margaret, ever the fighter, came right back to take the second set 6/1. The final set was a survival battle. The first six games saw four service-breaks. At 8-all Louise found herself 0/40 on her own service, only to serve her way out of trouble and then hold on to win the match 10/8, 1/6, 10/8.

After a brief interval the two Finalists (1) were back on court as a team to retain their Doubles title against fellow Americans Gussie Moran and Pat Todd (2), 8/6, 7/5. By now Louise had played sixty-nine games on that last Saturday. Her day was not yet done. She and John Bromwich (1), the holders of the Mixed Doubles, had again got to the Final where they were to meet South Africans Eric Sturgess and Sheila Summers (4). It became another marathon, going on so long and so late into the gathering dusk that it seemed it would overrun the traditional Wimbledon Ball. Sturgess and Summers won 9/7, 9/11, 7/5. On that day Louise had played a total of 117 games and had only just failed to win the triple crown for the second successive year.

It was not only serves, volleys and a squirrel which caught the eye that year. The lace around Gussie Moran's panties gave fashion designer Ted Tinling his first real imprint and brought an added alertness to many a male eye.

In 1950 sixteen men were seeded in the singles for the first time. This was due to the open nature of the field. The winners for the two previous years, Schroeder and Falkenburg, were absent. The No. 1 seed in 1949, Pancho Gonzales, had turned professional. The 1946 and 1947 champions, Petra and Kramer, were already in the professional ranks. This was the only occasion since the abolition of the Challenge Round in 1922, in which the Men's Singles did not contain one previous winner.

Frank Sedgman was No. 1 seed, mainly because, having twice won the Australian title, he had also just won the French Championship. He was given a close run by left-handed Art Larsen (7), and even super athlete Frank was drained after the battle, which went 8/10, 5/7, 7/5, 6/3, 7/5. Larsen was one of those great Wimbledon characters who have done so much to make the Championships. He was called Tappy because of his extraordinary compulsion to tap everything. The tapping had to be carried out to his own series of 'Enigma' Variations involving a prescribed number of taps for any one day.

John Barrett illustrates this with a story from a particular French Championship. Coming into the dressing-room Barrett came across Larsen busily tapping. A shower and ten minutes later John found Tappy still tapping, this time rearranging his clothes in an obviously related sequence but unable it seemed to get the magic combination. 'Can I help you, Tappy?' asked John. 'It's OK,' replied Tappy. 'I'll get myself unhooked in a minute.' Tappy endeared himself to Wimbledon hearts not only for his quirks of behaviour but for his traditional style and fighting qualities. He was slightly built to the point of seeming frail.

Sedgman got through to the Final, coming back from being two sets down to Drobny in the semi-finals. The man he faced on the other side of the net in the Final was Budge Patty (5), debonair as ever, nose tilted. Patty's tennis sparkled like the vintage champagne of his adopted France. It carried him zestfully to victory in the Final. This was a lovely match to watch, the incisive serve–volley game of Sedgman and his twinkling footwork against the elegance and artistry of the sophisticated Patty.

Bromwich and Quist (2), one of the greatest combinations ever, won the Doubles. The Doubles quarter-final between Sedgman and McGregor (1) and Patty and Trabert, both unseeded pairs, played on a torrid No. 1 Court, produced a record second set won by the Americans 31/29. Patty and Sedgman, on opposite sides of the net, seemed to be trying to conserve their energies for their singles final the following day.

The Ladies' Singles presented the usual American mixture with a semi-final line-up of Louise Brough (1) v. Doris Hart (3) and Margaret du Pont (2) v. Pat Todd (4). Louise Brough won in straight sets against Doris Hart. Pat Todd, who was unlucky to be a contemporary of three great players, pushed Margaret du Pont to the extent of her powers before losing 6/8, 6/4, 6/8. The Brough–du Pont Final was a three-setter, but in the two sets which Louise won she dropped only two games and so won her third successive title. She completed her triple crown with Margaret (1) in the Doubles (again an all-American affair) against Doris Hart and Shirley Fry (2) and Eric Sturgess (1) in the Mixed Doubles.

8

MIGHTY LITTLE MO
1951-5

1951 When Doris Hart (3) won match-point against Shirley Fry to gain the 1951 Ladies' Singles title, the Centre Court crowd and tennis fans everywhere experienced deep pleasure. For they knew that the road to victory, seldom easy, had been particularly hard for Doris. To start with, it was something of a miracle that she was playing tennis at all. As a baby in St Louis, Missouri, when taking her first faltering steps, she had fallen and hurt her knee. The tendons had been damaged and gradually the leg had been helplessly drawn up and all use of it lost.

With the help of friends, Doris's family by constant, tender massage brought life back to the leg. The family moved to Miami so that Doris could get the benefit of the sun. The next step was to provide exercise, so elder brother Bud took Doris to the local park to play tennis. It was a rare day when people using the park did not see them there.

In 1935 Doris and her brother had a particularly interested spectator – Slim Herbert, a tennis professional at a big Miami hotel. Doris was then ten. Slim began coaching her. Two years later she had won her first tournament. Within four years Doris was US Junior Doubles Champion and she caused a sensation when, still only sixteen, she beat Pauline Betz, second only to Alice Marble in the American rankings. At seventeen, Doris became American Junior Champion and was sixth in the senior rankings.

Having got to the top Doris had to live with two all-time greats, Louise Brough and Margaret Osborne (later du Pont). Doris made light of the impediment resulting from that childhood accident, for although her footwork looked affected her game was one of grace and flowing strides.

Doris Hart was at her fluent best in 1951. She was seeded No. 3, and to get to the Final she had to dispose of Mlle J. Marcellin, a young French player of promise, Mrs H. Weiss of Argentina, Australia's Nancye Bolton, Britain's Jean Rinkel-Quertier and fellow Americans Nancy Chaffee (7) and in the semi-finals Beverly Baker (5).

Beverley, later Mrs Fleitz, at her first Wimbledon had become an immediate crowd favourite. With her pretty turned-up nose and happy smile she had a most engaging manner. Added to which she was a baseline driver of the old school – with the difference that her strokes were mirrored as she was ambidextrous. It was Beverley who had put out Margaret du Pont (2). Top seed and reigning champion, Louise Brough (1), showing signs of elbow trouble, had been beaten in the semi-final by Shirley Fry (4).

Having got to her third Wimbledon Singles Final, Doris Hart seemed more than determined to win it and she beat Shirley Fry in just over half an hour. Then, with Shirley as her partner and seeded No. 2 she took the Ladies' Doubles title from the holders, Louise Brough and Margaret du Pont (1), in a hard-fought match 6/3, 13/11. Doris completed the triple crown when she and Frank Sedgman (2) won the Mixed Doubles.

As a result of the somewhat questionable long list of seeds in the previous year, 1951 saw the list for the men cut to ten. The main seeds were the holder, Budge Patty (4), the man he had defeated, Frank Sedgman (1), Drobny (2) and Larsen (3). Two American newcomers to Wimbledon were also seeded, Herbie Flam (5) and Dick Savitt (6).

Flam, the Paul Newman of tennis players, with hunched and self-deprecating look, got to the quarter-finals without dropping a set. There he met Sedgman. The Australian took the first two sets 6/2, 6/1. Flam then gave notice of his fine fighting qualities, took the third set 6/3 and, with two breaks of Sedgman's feared service, took the fourth set 6/4 to square the match. In the final set Flam, always a tenacious defender, broke Sedgman's service three more times to win an 'upset' victory. He then lost in the semi-final to another serve–volley specialist, Dick Savitt. Savitt was tall, dark and striking, both of looks and with his long sweeping forehand. In the Final, he outhit another big-game player, Australia's Ken McGregor (7).

The year provided the finest tennis hour for Britain's great favourite and loyal tennis servant, Tony Mottram, who in the third round beat the No. 2 seed Drobny. The match presented the Centre Court crowd with a dilemma. Drobny was an adopted favourite. Mottram was a home-born one. The crowd swayed Tony's way and finally urged him through an 8/6 final set. Mottram, like so many of the promising pre-war players, had lost his best years during the war, when he was a bomber pilot. He had a big game, particularly suited to Wimbledon's fast grass, and with full development of early promise could well have won the title.

1952 was a significant year in tennis history. Three all-time greats made their first appearances at Wimbledon – Maureen Connolly (2) ('Little Mo'), Lew Hoad and Ken Rosewall. Maureen is the only player to have achieved a perfect Wimbledon record since the Challenge Round was abolished. She came, she saw, she conquered – three years running. She then had a tragic riding accident and never played at Wimbledon again.

She was primarily a baseline player, but her accuracy was so unerring and her drives so fierce as they sought out the lines, that she put her opponents under almost continual pressure. She had a huge competitive instinct and at the slightest sign of danger would raise her sights and lessen still further the margin of error. Her drives on either wing became withering and occasionally

Herbie Flam, the Paul Newman of the game.

Frank Sedgman, Champion 1952, one of the fastest reflex players at the net.

Vic Seixas, 1953
Champion, said, 'A
true Champion
comes back to win it
twice.' Like many, he
failed in attempting
it.

Mighty 'Little Mo'
Connolly ranging her
forehand.

she put in a delicate surprise drop-shot. When she was in high mood, the crowd loved to watch her bobbing head, for as soon as a point was finished she immediately turned and marched briskly back to position, her head nodding like that of a foraging chicken. Most lovers of the game give her premier place since 1946 and many feel that she would have raised her game to beat any greats who came before or after her.

Maureen was the most sensational thing to happen to lawn tennis since Suzanne Lenglen. As an eleven-year-old she had been spotted playing on a public court in San Diego, California, by Wilbur Folson, who used to coach youngsters. Wilbur saw the potential in the girl with the curly hair and sparkling eyes and persuaded Mrs Connolly to let him coach Maureen. Almost immediately he made a radical change in her game, getting her to switch from left- to right-handed.

Maureen then came under the guidance of the top tennis coach in Southern California – Eleanor 'Teach' Tennant. Her progress was breathtaking. At thirteen she became the youngest girl to win the National Junior Championships; two years later she was ranked ten in the senior ratings; in August 1951, when only sixteen, she became America's youngest Wightman Cup player, beating Britain's No. 3, Kay Tuckey. The sensations continued, growing in size and in reaction. Nine days later, playing in the American Championships, Maureen knocked out Doris Hart. In the Final against Shirley Fry, sixteen-year-old Maureen took the first set 6/3, lost the second 1/6 and came back to win the decider.

At Wimbledon in her first match she beat Britain's Mrs C.G. Moeller without needing to take off her cardigan. But she did have to struggle in a fourth round match against attractive Sue Partridge. Here was a player with all the natural graces of beauty and stroke production, but lacking that essential killer instinct, a fault of so many British players. It was a lovely match, with the new phenomenon getting home only by 6/3, 5/7, 7/5. Little Mo also dropped a set in her quarter-final against Thelma Long (7) of Australia. These were the only two sets she was ever to lose at Wimbledon. She reached the Final by beating Shirley Fry (3).

Champion Doris Hart (1) looked vulnerable in her early matches, and was beaten in the quarter-finals in a long wavering match by Pat Todd (5), who in turn went out to Louise Brough (4).

The Final between seventeen-year-old Little Mo and the great Louise, who was conceding some twelve years, was eagerly awaited. Few thought that Maureen, even though she was reigning American champion, could sustain the high pitch she had reached at her first Wimbledon. She did. But how Louise fought to regain the crown she had worn so nobly. At one set down and 2/5 in the second, Louise was 0–40 facing three match-points. She saved them all and a fourth in the following game. But, at the fifth, after a thrilling rally, she was beaten by Little Mo's forehand which flashed across court, past her own. So Maureen, who had been given the nickname 'Little Mo' after the American battleship *Mighty Mo*, had found the range with her big guns to sink all opposition.

Lew Hoad and Ken Rosewall had been heralded as prodigies and, under the firm management of Harry Hopman, they quickly made their marks. Rosewall lost in the second round, but Hoad survived to give Drobny (2) a real fright in the fourth before going down in a match of big serves and ricocheting volleys.

In the doubles, Hoad and Rosewall had the Centre Court in a roaring fervour of delight, when in a five-set third round match they fought off a match-point to go on and beat the highly experienced pair, Mulloy and Savitt (2). In a match of many memories, that tense final set produced one shot which was unforgettable. Hoad was serving at 6/5. On the first point – vital at that stage – Rosewall, lobbed by one of his tall opponents with a perfect pitch to the baseline and with the ball running away from him, sprinted after the ball, and caught up with it just before the stop-netting. His nimbly adjustable foot-work placed him at the nth millisecond in perfect position to swivel and bring all the contra-rotating force of his body into a scintillating top-spin backhand which flew dipping at around shoulder height straight down the middle, splitting Mulloy and Savitt as if they had been straw figures. Like the audience, they could only stand, stare, wonder and laugh outright. The youngsters got through another round before falling to Seixas and Sturgess (4). They had not been able to emulate the feats of Little Mo. But they had served full warning of what was to come.

In the Singles Drobny, having survived Hoad's challenge, had two gruelling wins – each in five sets – over McGregor (5) and Flam (6) to reach his second Final. Mervyn Rose (3), that gifted left-hander and fine doubles player from Australia, beat an unconvincing Savitt (4), the holder, in five sets and then fell to Sedgman (1).

Sedgman v. Drobny in the Final. Both were previously defeated finalists. Both were determined that this would be their year. Drobny had beaten Sedg-man a few weeks before in the Final of the French Championships. But at Wimbledon Sedgman emerged victorious because, in yet another battle of services, he had the more commanding net-play for support. This was the last time that Wimbledon crowds were to see Sedgman at his best for, with the title to his name, he could no longer deny the beckoning sirens of the professional game.

Sedgman's win interrupted a long run of American success, which was renewed in 1953 when Vic Seixas (2) won from a field in which Ken Rosewall (1), on the strength of having won the Australian and French titles, had the signal honour of being seeded No. 1 when only eighteen and at only his second Wimbledon. However, in the quarter-finals he became the second in a row of three seeded players to be beaten by the sensation of the Championships – Kurt

Nielsen of Denmark, who reached the Final unseeded, to equal the feat of Wilmer Allison.

Hoad (6) also reached the quarter-finals where he took Seixas (2) to a 9/7 final set – here we saw the boy out of sorts, looking a little sulky while some of the corners were rubbed off him. The semi-final in which Seixas beat Rose (8) was a marathon of seventy-one games but was overshadowed by *the* marathon.

Drobny (2), having failed in two Finals and with the years slipping by, was determined that 1953 should be *his*. His great friend Patty (12), the 1950 Champion, stood in his way in the third round. The resulting clash was not only the match of the year, but till then probably the best ever played at Wimbledon, setting up a new record of ninety-three games lasting four hours twenty minutes. It began at five o'clock and ended in the twilight at 9.20 pm.

The drama – which developed quickly and was sustained on an impossible note for an impossible length of time – was a truly titanic struggle, such as was waged by the heroes of ancient legends. The final score, 8/6, 16/18, 3/6, 8/6, 12/10, indicates the level of the battle. The match was played to the fullest powers of both men. It was all a question of who was at the extreme elastic stretch of his ability and stamina at any one moment. Three times in the fourth set and again three times in the fifth, Patty held match-points. Each time Drobny countered him.

The winning effort probably cost Drobny the Championship for, although he survived two more rounds, he was ripe with leg weariness (he was hampered by a damaged blood vessel and by blisters on hands and feet) to fall to the bludgeoning of Nielsen's big game. In the Final the limited talent, and perhaps the nerve, of the great Dane were exposed by the more flexible and polished play of Vic Seixas who, after a tough first set, won in three. Hoad and Rosewall, already Australian and French Doubles Champions, deservedly won the Wimbledon title and went on to complete the Doubles grand slam in the United States.

On their way to the Wimbledon title they had a hectic time against two men who made up the most unusual ingredient of the Wimbledon scene at that time – the Austrian doubles combination of Huber and Redl. Huber was the Danny Kaye of tennis – a red-headed clown.

His playing distinction was his fantastic acrobatic agility, particularly at the net, where his headlong dives brought off spectacular coups and compensated for his partner's slight lack of mobility. His favourite crowd-pleasing trick was to bite the ball which had offended.

Redl was fair, balding and getting on in tennis maturity. His distinction was that he dismissed completely the loss of his left arm. He served by throwing up the ball from his racket and still managed to provide a most effective delivery. His balance was remarkable.

Between 1949 and 1953 Huber and Redl regularly won through a round or two and then in 1953 they reached the quarter-finals and gave a most lively display before going down in four sets to Hoad and Rosewall. The austere Redl gave the impression that he regarded Huber's antics, which in response to the crowd had become more exaggerated, as distasteful. Whether true or not, although both continued to come to Wimbledon, they did not again play as a pair.

Women's Champion, Maureen Connolly (1), looked the part all the way. Her final with Doris Hart (2) goes down as a Wimbledon classic. She won it 8/6, 7/5. Both players were at their peak and both felt afterwards that it was probably the best game of their lives. In the first set Maureen led 5/3, but nervously double-faulted twice. However, at 7/6 she had Doris Hart 0–40. Doris saved two set-points but at the third put her forehand out.

Connolly dropped the opening game of the second set, uncharacteristically making three mistakes, a reaction to that thrilling first set. However, she quickly took two services from Doris to lead 3/1, then dropped her own and games went with service to 5/5. At 4/4 Doris had a heaven-sent chance to break when she had two advantages in a game of six deuces on Maureen's service. But Little Mo, as always when danger reared, hit her way out of trouble. She went to 6/5 and then won Doris's service to love.

The calibre of Doris Hart's performance in this match is measured by her winning eleven games from the Champion. Up to the Final Maureen had lost only eight in five matches. Doris then shared in two Doubles titles, retaining the Women's with Shirley (1) and the Mixed, this time with Vic Seixas (1).

The following year Maureen (1) emphasized what a great Champion she was, retaining her title again with the loss of only nineteen games. She beat Margaret du Pont (5) 6/1, 6/1 in the quarter-finals, Betty Pratt (8) by the same score in the semis and yielded only seven games to Louise Brough (4) in the Final which she won 6/2, 7/5. That persistent British player, Angela Mortimer (6), was a-peeping through the green for the first time, reaching the quarter-finals.

The other outstanding event of the year was the success of Jaroslav Drobny in his third Final and after eleven attempts in sixteen years. Stung by being seeded only 11 out of 12, Drob blasted his way through Arkinstall, Torben Ulrich, Lennart Berglein, Phillipe Washer and, sensationally, Lew Hoad (2) – all in straight sets. He then met Budge Patty (7), and hearts bled for them after the epic marathon of the previous year and the toll it had taken of them. This time, Drobny won in four sets.

In the other half Rosewall (3) ran into no difficulty until the semi-finals where he met US Marine Tony Trabert (1), the American Champion and lately victor in Paris. Tony was following in the steps of many recent American champions, establishing himself before making a Wimbledon bid. Against Rosewall, Trabert had the slight edge after three sets, but then in the last two 'the Little Master' romped away 6/1, 6/1.

So to the Final and to the drama. Rosewall's genius was slightly subdued and his backhand was not the superb, reliable weapon everyone had come to expect. Drobny also made mistakes. But he also hit many glorious winners. His big serve and smash were much in evidence, so too was the delicate drop-shot touch he delighted in. Against this attack Rosewall deployed his full defensive dexterity, using spin and float in a varied mixture of shots. When Drobny led 2/1 he broke for 5/3 in the fourth, served for the match at 5/4 but was broken back and games went with service to 7/7. At 30–30 on Rosewall's service Ken netted a *backhand*.

At this crucial break-point the gods finally came down on Drobny's side. He played a backhand and got a dead net-cord. Rosewall's response was to play like a man possessed. With Drobny serving for the match, but at 15–30, Ken hit a marvellous running forehand cross-court drive, falling over in doing so, and forced 15–40. Drobny saved one break-back point with a smash and was lucky on the second with a questionable line call. He followed with an ace and took the title at his first match-point.

Wimbledon euphoria that day was complete. Everybody, but everybody, had wanted Drob to win. He had tried for so long. He was obviously such a nice guy and the women adored him. Seldom has a player so had the crowd on his side. A Rosewall error would bring applause which at times would spatter out shamefacedly. Little did anyone there that day think that years later they would twice be willing Rosewall to do the same thing and in the same situation. Then it seemed that a Wimbledon title was coming fast towards him.

1955 After Drobny's triumph in 1954, his peak had been reached and he was seeded only sixth in 1955. He got through to the quarter-finals where he went out to Tony Trabert (1). Trabert then won in straight sets against Patty (7), conqueror of young terror Hoad (4). Rosewall (2) came serenely through to the semi-final. Here he met Kurt Nielsen, victor in a five-set quarter-final over the gifted Nikki Pietrangeli. Pietrangeli was a delightful stroke-player with considerable tactical guile. His face and figure brought to mind a medieval cherub. But many an opponent who fell to his particular genius saw him in a different light. For Italy he was to achieve a Davis Cup record unlikely ever to be beaten – 119 victories in 164 rubbers.

Playing Rosewall, Nielsen clearly remembered his success against the Little Master in 1953, when he hit his approach shots down the middle and came to the net, making it difficult for Rosewall to play his favourite passing shots decisively. He pursued the same tactics and with the same result; for the *second* time he had reached the Final unseeded – a record which could stand for ever.

Finalists, Trabert and Nielsen, had similar games, the big serve followed by the clinching volley. But Trabert's had more depth, with a serious repertoire of strokes. He was moulded on the same pattern as Jack Kramer. Both were tennis machines with Trabert at his best almost Kramer's equal. His weakness was a long backswing on his forehand, which could be hurried into error. On

Beverly Baker (Mrs Fleitz), finalist in 1955, the most graceful ambidextrine Wimbledon has seen.

the day Nielsen lacked the inspiration he had found in beating Rosewall. Trabert won 6/3, 7/5, 6/1 at his second Wimbledon attempt and equalled the record of Hadow and Budge in winning the title without losing a set. He was one of the few players to possess a top-spin lob on forehand and backhand – an invaluable asset. His winning shot against Nielsen was a backhand cross-court top-spin lob which landed right on the line.

With Little Mo so sadly removed by her riding accident from her rightful place on the Centre Court, Doris Hart was the natural No. 1 seed with thrice champion Louise Brough at No. 2. In the semi-finals Louise met Darlene Hard (6). Darlene brought something new to Wimbledon. The crowd had mixed views on her extrovert manner on court but most people were taken with her vivacity. She was always making gestures, slapping her thigh, talking, and was a natural reactor to any given situation, such as shaking hands with a linesman she had crashed into – in the manner of a Borotra. She played a strong, masculine-type game, occasionally rent by a gale of errors. Louise Brough beat her only 6/3, 8/6 to reach her seventh final.

In the other semi-final, ambidextrous Beverley Fleitz (3) gave a superb display to beat Doris Hart. With her shots speeding on either wing and to such length, she stood comparison with Maureen Connolly at her best. Indeed, she had been the only player to beat Maureen in 1954. Doris Hart (1), the reigning US Champion, did not win one game in the second set. Beverley's pace withered her game. Beverley Fleitz not only looked the complete player on the day, she was lovely with it. She was one of the most attractive movers in the ladies' game.

The Final presented the free-hitting Beverley Fleitz against Louise Brough, the majestic ex-Champion. Louise was always prone to tighten up at important points but had a greater breadth of stroke and experience at her command, which just saw her through a keenly fought struggle. In the sixth game of the second set, for example, it was only after nine deuces and five advantages to Fleitz that Brough wrong-footed her near-exhausted opponent with a backhand slice down the line to lead 4/2. This was a major turning point and Louise went on to win her fourth Singles title, 7/5, 8/6.

The year was also memorable for the performances of the British girls in the doubles. In the first round Jennifer Middleton and Doreen Spiers knocked out No. 1 seeds, Doris Hart and Mrs Davidson. They lost in the third round to Fay Muller and Jenny Hoad, but the Final was an all-British affair, the first time since 1929. In it Angela Mortimer and Anne Shilcock (4) beat Shirley Bloomer and Pat Ward (3), 7/5, 6/1.

For many even more memorable was the grace in form and in dress of Italy's Lea Pericoli. Ted Tinling must have been delighted with her as a model for his frilly creations.

9

WALTZING MATILDA AND QUEEN MARIA 1956–60

In 1956 the Australian 'tennis twins', Lew Hoad and Ken Rosewall, who had threatened so much since their arrival as seventeen-year-olds in 1952, fulfilled that threat when they justified their first and second seeding by reaching the Final. Hoad had straight set wins until his quarter-final with Mal Anderson. Anderson, a rangy player from Queensland, had a big game and gave Hoad a good four-set fight, after which he had to receive treatment for sunstroke. Anderson next year caused a big surprise by being the first man to win the American title unseeded.

Hoad looked in ominously good form in disposing of Ham Richardson (6), who had caused a sensation at his first Wimbledon in 1951 by beating reigning champion, Budge Patty, but had then faded. This year Patty (4) had fallen in the second round to a brilliant No. 1 Court display by Britain's Bobby Wilson, one of the finest classic stroke-makers tennis has known. Wilson had a habit of springing good wins like this at Wimbledon but then going out next round, in this case to Neale Fraser. If Wilson had had the will-to-win of Fred Perry he would surely have been the first Englishman to follow in his footsteps. More cheer for Britain when John Barrett, who has done so much for home tennis, had the distinction in his first round match of being the only man to take a set from Rosewall on his way to the Final.

So the twins at last met in their only Wimbledon Final, with Hoad, having won the Australian and French titles, going for the grand slam. Each knew the other's game well and they were almost perfect examples of complete opposites. Hoad was strongly built, chunky with a mighty forearm and a wrist of steel which allowed him to play almost any shot from any position with maximum force and control. On his day, when in a mood of high concentration, nobody could live with him. But he was a lazy player, as so many of the supremely gifted are, and he needed the spur of danger on an important occasion to bring out the best in him.

In contrast to Hoad's blond, forceful good looks, Rosewall, older by three weeks, was dark and always tended to look shy and self-deprecating, with a curious habit between rallies of appearing to droop suddenly. But he had a steely resolution, superb strokes, particularly his famous backhand. And his return of service was renowned. An aspiring Wimbledon player, an admirer of Rosewall's, seeking advice asked the 'Little Master', 'What do you do when you are having trouble with your service returns?' Muscles, scratching his head, replied, 'I wouldn't know about that.'

His one real weakness was his lack of power in service and overhead. He partly overcame this by his length and accuracy and in later years as a professional added more power.

The weakness was always surprising in one who otherwise was so perfect, and was the most mercurial and quickest reacting volleyer the game has seen. But in his autobiography with Peter Rowley, Rosewall revealed that as a boy he was a natural left-handed thrower. What a player Rosewall might have been had he started serving left-handed, for the service is the action of throwing the racket head at the ball.

On that Final day of 1956 it was just Hoad, but only just, in four richly entertaining sets and *because* it was a Wimbledon Final. Hoad was the supreme player for the supreme occasion. Rosewall subsequently reversed the Wimbledon result when he beat Hoad in the American Final, so denying him an epic grand slam. It was inevitable, and fitting, that Hoad and Rosewall (1) won the Doubles, repeating their 1953 success. It was Rosewall's last Centre Court appearance for eleven years, for he turned professional after his American Forest Hills success.

In the Women's Championship 1956 goes down as the year Shirley Fry (5) came good and Angela Buxton (6) combined fortune with persistent courage to become the first Briton to reach a Singles Final since 1939. Beverly Fleitz (2) reached the quarter-finals but withdrew in the words of the *Daily Telegraph* 'for delicate and happy reasons'. This gave Pat Ward, who had been at the top of her form in beating Angela Mortimer (3), a semi-final against Angela Buxton who won well.

Angela Buxton had reached match-point against Shirley Fry only a week or two before in a Wightman Cup match. But in the Final Shirley Fry, of the big grin, would not be denied. She had had to live in the shadows of the great American tennis queens, Louise Brough, Margaret du Pont and Doris Hart, and so was all the more determined to make the most of this opportunity.

This then was the end of an era and the strain of great American champions had passed its peak. But Shirley Fry well deserved her honour, even though it was an interim year. On her way to the Final she beat Louise Brough (1), the reigning title-holder and Althea Gibson (4), the Champion-to-be. Angela Buxton completed a fine Wimbledon when, partnered by Althea Gibson (3), she won the Women's Doubles.

1957   The following year Althea Gibson became a Wimbledon Champion in her own right, the first black player to win any Wimbledon title, and well she deserved to do. The sixteen-year-old Christine Truman blazed a British comet's trail whose startling light lit the Wimbledon scene, especially the Centre Court, with a patriotic glow. As a result she was chosen for the Wightman Cup team – the youngest ever on either side.

Bob Wilson, flying trapeze artist.

A foregone final: Hoad and Rosewall won their second title against Pietrangeli and Sirola, 1956.

The Queen came to Wimbledon on the final Saturday to pay her first visit as monarch. It was a scorchingly hot day and the luncheon room was stifling. As ever the Wimbledon organization was equal to the problem. Ice blocks were put in front of the fans and a cool lunch was enjoyed by all.

On court, Althea Gibson (1), in the Final at her second Wimbledon attempt, kept *her* cool to beat Darlene Hard (5) 6/3, 6/2. She was a good Champion, having the now accepted typical American big serve–volley game. Reminiscent of Doris Hart in her movements but without Doris's full range of strokes, Althea was tough and athletic and this was how she played her tennis. Her style and her competitive instinct were born of a background which had seen her as a thirteen-year-old playing street baseball and paddle ball (a form of small court tennis) in Harlem. How different from the home life of other tennis queens. With so little going for her it is not surprising that Althea took longer than most to make her way in the tennis world. It is a great testimony to her that she kept fighting, to make her breakthrough in her thirtieth year and win both Wimbledon and the US title.

Louise Brough (2), despite her lapse the previous year, was given second seeding but lost to Darlene Hard in the quarter-finals. This was her last Singles appearance, the end of twelve glorious years which left grateful memories. Angela Mortimer (7) unexpectedly fell in the third round to America's Karol Fageros, 'the golden girl of tennis', at her first Wimbledon. She became famous for her golden panties, outglittering even Gussie Moran.

Christine Truman quickly made herself the darling of the Centre Court. Still only a schoolgirl, she had a Diana the Huntress look as she swept into the net in her serve–volley game. There was something so fresh and appealingly English about her, and the crowd took her to their hearts as the Joan of Arc of British tennis. For she was succeeding when little success came Britain's way. Her first two wins were excusable temerity, but in the fourth round she met Shirley Bloomer (3), one of Britain's most experienced players, and disposed of her in straight sets.

By now all Britain was in her triumphant wake and at times overtaking her, expecting miracles. They were granted one in the quarter-finals when Christine beat Mrs Betty Pratt, a highly experienced player from the United States. Christine won a long match 9/7, 5/7, 6/4. The fairy story ended when Althea Gibson doused Christine's tempestuous attack to the tune of 6/1, 6/1. But Britain now had a heroine and one whom they felt could grasp the prize. Christine's appearance was innocent, but behind it lay a strong determination.

1957 was unquestionably Hoad (1) again and Hoad all the way. The challenge to him was not as strong as before. Rosewall had gone to the professional ranks, Seixas (6) was declining, and Richardson (3), who might have provided a tough Final opponent, went out in a sensational first round defeat to workmanlike Luis Ayala of Chile. Herbie Flam (7), Finalist in Paris, was beaten by a new star from Australia, Ashley Cooper (2), who also disposed of

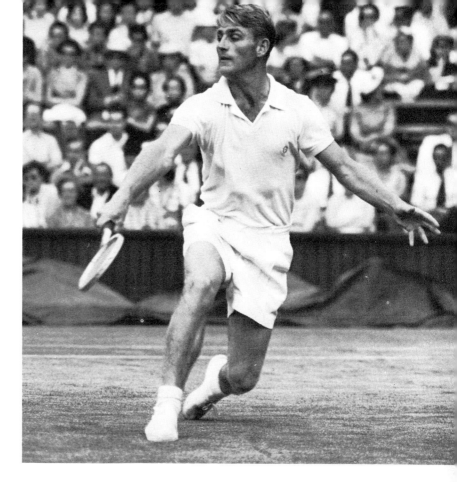

Hoad knows where
it's going.

Fraser follows
through. He won the
Wimbledon title in
1960.

the rising Neale Fraser (5) in the semi-finals. This was further illustration of what was for many years an almost invariable rule for the top American and Australian players, that when two of the same country met the senior ranker nearly always won. In this instance Cooper, having lost the first set, needed a 14/12 second set to affirm his superior ranking.

Two leading British players, left-hander Bill Knight, more at home on the hard court with his heavy top-spin forehand and chipped backhand, and Bobby Wilson both reached the last sixteen. Knight fell to Flam, and Wilson to Sven Davidson (4), who was reaching his peak. Another British hope, Mike Davies, the Welsh boy who started playing tennis to prove that he could do anything better than his brother and hitch-hiked from tournament to tournament in his early days, had a good Wimbledon, defeating Arkinstall and Owen before going out in five sets to Neale Fraser.

The Final saw Hoad at his devastating best. His power, ferocious yet controlled, was awesome. Cooper was dismissed 6/2, 6/1, 6/2 in fifty-seven minutes. Hoad's mastery was so complete, not only over his opponent but over his own skills, that he was simply irresistible. In terms of skating or diving he would have gained maximum points. Hoad was again supreme on the supreme occasion. He was not consistent, because of his innate laziness, but had the depth of skill and stamina to see him through any ordinary encounter without great effort. However, when his own pride was at stake, as in a Wimbledon Final, he went into overdrive and stayed there. Hoad then joined Rosewall in the professional ranks.

1958 The following year Ashley Cooper (1) was again in the Final. This time it was his turn to humble a lower-ranked fellow countryman, Neale Fraser (4), in a four-set repeat of their 1957 semi-final. It was a big serve–volley match, very like Cooper's battle against another Australian left-hander, Mervyn Rose (3), in the semi-finals.

Cooper had to work hard for his title. He was in difficulties in the first round against Britain's Geoff Owen, struggled through a fourth round marathon against hard-hitting South African left-hander, Abe Segal, and was taken to five sets in the quarter-finals by Bobby Wilson. Fraser had a very hard quarter-final against Sweden's Sven Davidson, a handsome, dark player who would surely have gone further if he had not turned aside to concentrate on his studies. Against the battling Dane, Kurt Nielsen (6), in the semi-finals, Fraser had won in four sets, losing a mammoth third 17/19.

Althea Gibson (1) had stormy seas to weather in retaining her title. In a third round match against vivacious Mexican, Yola Ramirez, she won the first set only 9/7. Althea was more commanding in beating Lorraine Coughlan of Australia 6/0, 6/2. She then met Shirley Bloomer (5) in a replay of their Wightman Cup match of two weeks earlier when Althea had won comfortably 6/3, 6/4.

To digress, in her Wightman Cup double, partnered by Christine Truman,

Wimbledon concourse. The
record – 37,290 – was set on
Friday 27 June 1975.

Althea Gibson – a determined
Champion 1957–8

Miss Bloomer had surprised herself and the crowd when her petticoat slid to the ground. With the greatest aplomb, she stepped gracefully out of it, picked it up, carried it to the umpire's chair and resumed playing. It was in this same Wightman Cup tie that Christine played the greatest game of her life, to beat the Champion, Althea Gibson, and gain revenge for her semi-final defeat at Wimbledon the previous year. This unlocked the heavily barred door to a famous British victory. Christine relates how sportingly Althea took defeat.

In the Championships Althea Gibson was given a fight by Shirley Bloomer before winning 6/3, 6/8, 6/2 to get to the semi-finals. There she conquered unseeded Ann Haydon. Christine Truman (2) went out in the fourth round to a petite but determined Mimi Arnold, who won 10/8, 6/3. This gave the lively brunette from Hungary, Suzy Kormoczi (6), a run to the semi-final. She came up against Angela Mortimer, who had put paid to the old champion Mrs du Pont in a stirring three-set quarter-final. Angela crushed Suzy 6/0, 6/1 in thirty-one minutes, and so reached the Final unseeded, the second woman to do so. The foundation of her victory was her impeccable driving length and a relentless capacity of return, which were too much for Suzy.

Two British players in the semi-finals and one in the Final was a post-war record. In that Final Angela Mortimer brought the fighting best out of Althea Gibson. At 5/4 in the first set Angela had set point at 40–30, when Althea played a fine forehand deep into the backhand corner to save it. She eventually won 8/6, 6/3 with a run of six successive games, her sustained attack finally breaking down the pinpoint accuracy and length of Angela's driving. Althea Gibson took the Doubles with Maria Bueno (1) and just missed the triple crown when she and Kurt Nielsen (2) were beaten in the final of the Mixed Doubles, by Bob Howe and Lorraine Coughlan, 6/2, 13/11, in one of the most exciting matches of the tournament.

In her Wimbledon début Maria Bueno (4), although beaten by Ann Haydon in the quarter-finals, had caught the crowd's imagination and admiration with her catlike grace and majestic strokes.

1959   Wimbledon 1959 provided good weather and the first Russian entry. There had been concern over who should be accepted since the Russians had not played internationally and their form was not known. Fortunately their officials (and there were always some of those around) had no objections to their playing through the Qualifying Tournament. A. Potatnin and Tomas Lejus qualified in the Men's Singles but did not survive the first round. Nor did Anna Dmitrieva in the Women's. But they did enough to show that Russia meant tennis business.

It was also unique as the year in which South America won both singles titles. Maria Bueno (6) fulfilled the tremendous potential she had shown the year before and, although she dropped the first set to Miss Dittmeyer in the second round – a lapse she repeated against Mimi Arnold in the third round – in her last three matches against Edda Buding, Sally Moore (7) and Darlene Hard

Christine Truman, the British
St Joan, in her most famous
victory, 1958, against Althea
Gibson, the reigning
Wimbledon Champion. It
turned the key for Britain's
Wightman Cup win.

Maria Bueno. Olé!

(4) she looked every bit the peerless Champion. Rarely, if ever, has such physical beauty of movement been combined with such marvellous strokes, to which timing gave ferocious power, allied usually to impeccable length. She looked like a panther hunting for the kill. At peak form her game was imperious, all she lacked was Little Mo's consistency.

Maria came from a well-to-do family, whose apartment was opposite the Sao Paulo club. From her earliest days in the pram she could hear the sound of tennis balls. Later, qualifying as a schoolteacher, her schedule for the month preceding her first world tour was as follows: 2 am rise and study; 5.30 am tennis practice; 7.15 am bath, breakfast; 9 am school; 4 pm home for meal, more studying until bed at 11.00. In that month, Maria, who did not appear to have much spare weight, lost 17 lb. Maria was not just an inspired and beautiful player. She had a champion's mettle. She also made sure that she knew what to expect in a match by closely studying her likely opponents. In the Final she beat Darlene Hard (4). Angela Mortimer (2) and Ann Haydon (8) both went out in the quarters. Christine Truman (1), the new and youngest-ever French lady champion, lost no admirers when she lost in the fourth round.

The first round of the Men's Singles produced three sensations when 1950 champion, Budge Patty, was beaten by J.A. Douglas of USA; Pietrangeli (3) went out to another American, Butch Buchholz, who was at his first Wimbledon, and heart-throb Drobny, the 1954 winner, was beaten in a marathon by that stylist from Great Britain, Alan Mills, 14/12, 3/6, 10/8, 8/6. Mills was playing excellent tennis at this time and, had he been of sterner temperament, might well have gone far in the game. As it was he progressed this year to the last sixteen, where he met a tough little redhead called Laver, who became the third man in Wimbledon history to reach the Final unseeded.

Laver had a terrific match in the semi-finals with Barry MacKay (5) of the USA before winning 11/13, 11/9, 10/8, 7/9, 6/3 (87 games) second only in length to the Drobny/Patty marathon of 1953. Being a warm, dry year, long matches were the order of the day, with the fast, true surface favouring the serve–volleyers. Another long-winded match was Fraser's fourth round clash with the giant Italian, Orlando Sirola, which went to seventy-one games. This year was also significant for Roy Emerson (8), who was seeded for the first time and made a long run for home, which culminated with a fine quarter-final win over Bob Wilson (4).

However, Olmedo (1) put an end to Emerson's charge with a semi-final victory of three sets to love. Olmedo, Peruvian-born but playing for the United States, was rising rocket-like into the tennis stratosphere. Almost single-handed he had won the Davis Cup for the United States in Australia and had gone on to take the Australian title. For the present he had more boost than the man known as the Rocket – Rod Laver.

Credit for originating Laver's nickname goes to Harry Hopman, the famed Australian coach and team manager. When the skinny, freckled redhead from

Alex Olmedo, the puma of Peru.

Mike Davies, doubles finalist with Bobby Wilson in 1960.

Rockhampton, Queensland, was first presented to him, Harry said: 'Well, Rocket, let's see what you can do.' In the Final Rocket gave a good account of himself, and a warning for the future, but could not take a set from Olmedo. Olmedo followed this by getting to the Final of the American Championship, where he lost to Fraser and then turned professional. He had the unusual satisfaction, for a new boy in the pro ranks, of winning his first match – against Gonzales at that.

A sad note in an otherwise happy Wimbledon year was the sudden death in January of the All England Club's popular chairman, Dr Colin Gregory, who had succeeded King George VI's friend, Sir Louis Greig. Dr Gregory had been a notable player, who not only reached the Wimbledon Doubles Final in 1929 but in the same year had won the Australian Singles. In 1952 he made Davis Cup history when, in a tie with Yugoslavia, he forsook his role of non-playing captain to help win the important doubles.

1960   With Olmedo in the professional ranks, 1960 saw Fraser (1) given the top seeding, although Laver (3) had reached the Final in 1959. There were good reasons. Fraser was American Champion and, although beaten by Laver in the Australian Final, was still the official Australian No. 1, with Roy Emerson 2. At Wimbledon Laver was given third seeding and Emerson 6. He proved the Seeding Committee right when in the quarter-finals he beat Roy in four sets. Indeed, the Seeding Committee could congratulate itself. All the men's seeds reached their appointed quarter-final places and only two of the women's failed.

Krishnan (7) was the first Indian to reach a semi-final and did so again the following year. Barry MacKay (2) was unfortunate that it was a wet year, for he depended so much on fast courts for his big game. In the quarter-finals he met Pietrangeli (5) in a match probably decided by the first set, which went to the Italian 16/14. Pietrangeli charmed the Centre Court further with his delightful free game and took Laver to five sets in the semi-finals. Neale Fraser had few worries in reaching the Final, except in the quarter-finals where he met Butch Buchholz (8), who had made such a mark the year before. The American, leading Fraser 2/1, twisted an ankle at the beginning of the fourth set. Fraser at that point had survived three match-points, one of them when Butch netted a sitter from three yards.

The Final was a battle of left-handers, the first in Wimbledon history. Fraser's big serve and senior status gave him the edge over Laver but not without a hard fight 6/4, 3/6, 9/7, 7/5. It was not going to be long before the Rocket powered into orbit.

The Men's Doubles produced one particularly fine match, in which the unseeded Osuna and Ralston, having beaten the fourth seeds Pietrangeli and Sirola in five sets, played an inspired game in the semi-finals to beat the No. 2 seeds, Laver and Mark, 4/6, 10/8, 15/13, 4/6, 11/9 (eighty-six games). In the Final they met Britain's first pair, Davies and Wilson, who in the quarter-finals had beaten Emerson and Fraser (1), the Champions, in five sets. So the first Doubles Final between two unseeded pairs came about and, on the day, Osuna and Ralston were the sharper, winning 7/5, 6/3, 10/8. Osuna, at twenty-one was playing at his first full Wimbledon, having failed to qualify two years before, while seventeen-year-old Ralston was USA Junior Champion and making his first-ever Wimbledon visit.

In the Women's Championship Maria Bueno (1) was already riding high. She had won the previous American title, defeating Christine Truman in the Final. She cruised through her early rounds, beating as good a player as Angela Mortimer (5) 6/1, 6/1 to get to the semi-finals, where yet again she met the lance of St Joan Truman (3) tilting for Britain. Bueno was at her majestic best, producing a stream of classic strokes to take the first set 6/0. It says much for Christine's fighting spirit that she could come back to win the second set 7/5. Thereupon La Bueno reasserted her authority to win the third set 6/1.

A new name had appeared in the women's line-up, Karen Hantze of America, whose looks caught the eye and who, despite deceptively slow movements between points, had a sound all-court American game. In the quarter-finals she had taken Christine to three sets. Ann Haydon (4) reached her ordained semi-final for the second time, where she met the attractive South African, Sandra Reynolds (8), conqueror of Darlene Hard (2). Sandra got the better of Ann in three sets and so reached the Final.

In the Final, Champion Maria was given a searching examination, especially by Sandra's famous forehand. Nor was the challenger's backhand as defensive as usual, for it seemed to have been sharpened by the pressure put upon it. Sandra did not use her renowned backhand drop-shot as she had with such success against Ann Haydon. Probably wisely, for Maria Bueno was no less forceful in her volleys than in her ground strokes and she finished the first set 8/6 with three such superb shots.

The second set score of 6/0 was cruelly unjust to the fight put up by Sandra Reynolds. The third game, for example, went to nine deuces and five game-points on either side. When Maria won it after twelve minutes the South African's resistance crumbled and she won only three more points. That game also underlined just what a fighter Maria was. Even when right on top she would never yield a point. Her first great triumph in 1959 had enshrined her in the hearts of all Brazilians, and her successful defence of the title prompted the Sao Paulo authorities to honour her with a statue and a postage stamp.

Two greats of the past died in 1960. Dolly Lambert Chambers, seven times Champion, died on 7 January, aged eighty-one. On 27 June, the second Monday of the Championships, Lottie Dod died at the age of eighty-eight. Lottie, five times Champion before retiring unbeaten at twenty-one, went on to conquer in other sporting arenas. She was, in the judgement of many, the greatest woman all-rounder of all time.

MORTIMER, SMITH AND TRUMAN TOO 1961–5

1961 Rod Laver comes from a hardy background on the family cattle farm in Queensland. Living in the seaside town of Rockhampton he grew up in a tennis atmosphere. Family outings were normally in the form of taking part in tennis tournaments, with the Lavers collecting most of the prizes. Being short and wiry, Rod decided that he must master top-spin. He did this to such effect that he is one of the few players able to control any stroke at will and he possesses those two deadly weapons, the forehand and backhand top-spin lobs.

Like Lew Hoad, he has the ability to play any shot from any part of the court, and play it with force and penetration. He has a wrist of steel and the muscles on his racket forearm look almost twice the size of those on his right arm. Like Ken Rosewall he flourished under the coaching and team management of Harry Hopman, the man who guided, shaped and commanded the Australian squad. Stories of Hopman's strict routine and discipline were retailed with awe, stories of rigid curfews and spartan training. Certainly when it came to winning Hopman was single-minded. He could not have had better disciples than Rosewall and Laver, both dedicated to perfect fitness which allowed untrammelled expression of their genius. In Hoad, with his great natural strength and stamina, as well as brilliant inspiration, Hopman found a less compliant spirit.

Laver (2) had his worries on the way to the 1961 Final. That excellent French player, Pierre Darmon, who is a respected voice on the Professional Council, had an on day and took the Rocket all the way, as did Bungert, that skilful German touch player. Thereafter Laver fired on full power and easily beat Krishnan (7), who had reached the semi-final for the second year running. In doing so he had displayed all the delicate deftness and improvisation, which – like Cochet and Bergelin before him – he had made his hallmark.

In the Final against Chuck McKinley (8) Rod brought to bear all the authority of his experience of two previous finals, winning 6/3, 6/1, 6/4. Chuck ran down the baseline like a mechanical hare in his efforts to retrieve, throwing himself all over the place, falling, rolling over and still getting the ball back.

With four Britons, Knight, Sangster, Wilson and Taylor, in the last sixteen, home fans had more to cheer about from the men than at any time since the war. Sangster and Wilson survived to the quarter-finals. Wilson again produced

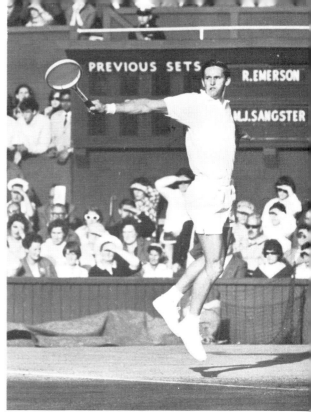

ABOVE Angela Mortimer, Wimbledon Champion 1961. Hers was the reward for patience, perseverance and practice.

ABOVE RIGHT Emmo rises to the occasion.

BELOW Easy come for once to Chuck McKinley, winner 1963.

one of his Wimbledon conjuring tricks (alas he was never able to perform a repeat in the same year) when he put out the Champion, Fraser, in four sets. Wilson then fell to McKinley. Sangster, with his big serve, started a gush of British optimism by sweeping aside Segal and Venezuela's Pimentel to reach the semi-final for the first time, where McKinley too was his downfall.

But it was the girls who in 1961 really delivered the goods for Britain. In the absence through illness of Maria Bueno, which cost her a possible hat-trick of titles, Angela Mortimer (7) and Christine Truman (6) made it an all-British Final. This was the first time such a thing had happened since those far-off, long-skirted days of 1914 when Mrs Lambert Chambers beat Mrs Larcombe, and Britain was certain of her first Singles title since Dorothy Round's win in 1937.

Both Angela and Christine had earned their places in the sun on that final Wimbledon Saturday by right of conquest over highly rated players. Angela (7), full of stern resolve and purpose, the edge of her concentration at its absolute peak and enhanced, she felt, by a temporary deafness, beat Sandra Reynolds (1) to reach the Final, coming from behind in both sets.

Christine Truman (6) caused the big shock in the quarter-finals when she beat Margaret Smith (2), the reigning Australian and French Champion. Still just eighteen, this was Margaret's first Wimbledon and her powerful all-round game, based on her fine physique, had made a big impression. In the deciding set Christine had to survive two match-points before getting through 3/6, 6/3, 9/7.

With two home players in the Final, the crowd had a rare dilemma. Who to favour? Angela Mortimer was well liked and admired for her patience, persistence and sheer resolution, qualities which had helped her turn comparatively weak strokes into commanding weapons. But, and it was a big but, Christine Truman, for the last four years, had been seen as Britain's leading standard-bearer, going forward to meet the foreign invader. So it was St Joan Truman who had most of the crowd with her.

Truman served first, but at 30/40 dropped her service and gave Angela Mortimer an immediate advantage which she held to 4/2, both players repeatedly saving break-points. Then Truman stormed into one of her famous attacks to take four games in a row for the set. At this point rain interrupted play for half an hour. On the restart both players dropped their first service games. At 4/3, Christine had a break-point which Angela saved with a backhand passing shot down the line. A double-fault by Angela gave Christine a second chance. Coming to the net to seize it she fell awkwardly and hurt her left thigh. Her natural sportsmanship saw her jump up and carry on. She had two more break-points. On the first she put a backhand out and on the second her forehand return of serve bounced once on top of the net before skipping sideways and out.

She was clearly affected by the fall, becoming sluggish and slow on the turn,

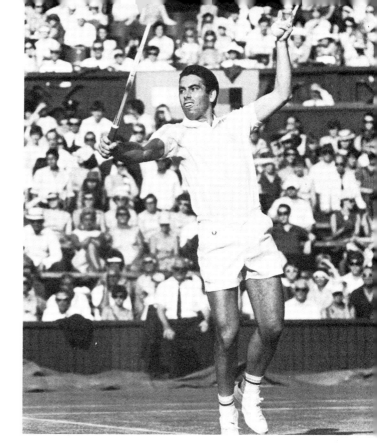

Santana waves the wand.

Margaret Court in for the kill.

and dropped the next two games for the set. Angela got off to a good start to lead 2/0 in the deciding set. Christine's fighting spirit gradually pulled back to somewhere near her best and in a see-saw finish six games in a row went against service. Then, at 6/5, Angela held her service to win the coveted title.

The gods had dealt both players difficult hands that day. To most of those watching it seemed certain that Christine, at the moment she fell, was on the way to a straight sets win and the title which her adoring fans wanted her so much to have. If she had got one of the two break-points after her fall she would probably have succeeded in holding her service for the match. To lose that game then, with the memory of the fall so fresh and still physically affecting her, took the keen edge off her game.

Equally Angela found herself suddenly with a chance to retrieve what had looked like a lost cause. But she still had the difficulty of playing a handicapped opponent, and of playing the right game which was not to ignore the injury but to play on it. The opportunity was there to stretch Christine. The situation demanded that she should. Being a fine match player she did. In the outcome she was a good Champion.

1962   The Women's Championship in 1962 saw the defeat in her first match of Margaret Smith (1) by Billie Jean Moffitt, her name and game drawing notice the previous year when she won the Doubles with Karen Hantze. It was to be the first of many Wimbledon battles between the two, Billie Jean winning this time by 7/5 in the final set. Defeat for Margaret was all the more surprising as she came to Wimbledon as holder of the Australian, Italian and French titles. Billie Jean, herself, went down in the quarter-finals to Ann Haydon, who reached the semi-finals for the third time, losing there to Karen Hantze, now Susman (8).

Karen's opponent in the Final was the Czech, Vera Sukova, who was the third woman to reach the Final unseeded, winning many friends on the way with her modestly endearing personality and determined game. In successive rounds she beat both Darlene Hard (2) and Maria Bueno (3), who were making their Wimbledon returns. In the Final nerves and a suspect ankle prevented the Czech girl from getting the best out of herself and she fell to the power of Karen Susman, recently married and playing with more conviction.

By now the Rocket had established his fame in his own name of Rod Laver. He was intent on equalling Donald Budge's 1938 record of winning the grand slam. He had already won the Australian and French titles. At Wimbledon in the fifth round he met Manuel Santana (6), whose inspiration was maturing with experience. The Spaniard gave the Champion a fright and the spectators marvellous entertainment, winning the first set 16/14 and leading 5/1 in the second. Up to that point Laver had lacked his Champion's authority, due largely to the magical play of the Spaniard, with his adroit lob-volleys – the most difficult stroke to play with precision. With his title in danger Laver's Champion spark flared and raised his game. He took four games in a row and eventually the set at 9/7, to level the match, and then continued his surge to win it. He saved his title and the grand slam by a narrow margin.

Laver's opponent in the Final was seeded to be Roy Emerson (2), who had a fine second round match against Bungert, losing the first two sets 13/15, 4/6 but, fit as ever, cantering through the next three. In the fourth round Emerson had to retire with an injured toe when 1/1 to Marty Mulligan, who went on to become the fourth unseeded man to reach the Final. There Marty found Laver at his ruthless best, the Champion holding his title 6/2, 6/2, 6/1.

Overall the Men's Championship had borne a distinctly Australian accent, with six of their players in the eight quarter-final places. Credit was due both to individual ability and its harnessing by Harry Hopman. Laver had been in four successive Wimbledon Finals, winning the last two. Had he remained an amateur there seemed to be nobody around to end his reign.

Three footnotes on 1962: Bob Hewitt, the balding, swarthy, doubles magician, originally Australian but who adopted South African nationality after marrying his beautiful Delaille, won the first of his four (so far!) Doubles titles. The second note records that great champion, Margaret du Pont, winner of three American and one Wimbledon singles titles, partnering Neale Fraser to win the Mixed Doubles – sixteen years after her first Wimbledon victory in the Women's Doubles, partnered by Louise Brough. Thirdly, Colonel Legg retired as Referee, having carried out this exacting duty with quiet and friendly firmness for twelve years. Perhaps the Colonel's most difficult assignment was in 1957 to remove the lady who decided to stage a one-woman peace demonstration on the Centre Court. This was just after the Ladies' Singles Final and when the Queen was in the Royal Box. There was momentary silence as many wondered if this was all part of the show. Then the short figure of Colonel Legg came to the rescue, advancing with long, jerky strides on the 'local disturbance'. Valiantly he tried to pull her off court. Weight for weight he was no match, but his resolution prevailed.

For Colonel Legg's successor, son-in-law Capt. Mike Gibson, 1963 was a difficult blooding, as it was for David Mills who had succeeded Col Macaulay as Secretary. It was a year of disastrous weather. Through adroit rearrangement the programme had caught up by the second Friday. However, on Saturday it rained all day and so all but the Men's Final (decided on Friday) were postponed until the Monday. This was the first time this had happened in thirty-six years.

Margaret Smith (1) was deservedly top women's seed and, despite attacks of her Centre Court nerves, she got through to the Final. Here she met Billie Jean Moffitt, who again provided upsets in beating Lesley Turner (2) and Ann Haydon (3), now Mrs Pip Jones, who had won through to her fifth semi-final. In the Final Billie Jean lost the first set. Audibly urging herself on, she rallied from 0/4 down in the second to lose it and the match 6/4. But she had done more than enough in getting through to the Final unseeded (the fourth woman to do so), and against Margaret, to establish her credentials for the future.

In the Men's draw it was a year of upsets, due partly to the wet weather and slower courts. Only three seeds reached the Men's quarter-finals, Emerson (1), Santana (seeded 2 by credit of his new French title), and McKinley (4). McKinley got through to the Final. There he met a tall, fair, gangling Australian, Fred Stolle, who had become the fifth man to reach the Final unseeded. In the Final McKinley found the slower court suited to his fantastic retrieving game. In typical all-American fashion he grabbed his chance and the match 9/7, 6/1, 6/4. He had the distinction of joining Budge and Trabert as the only men, since the Challenge Round was abolished, to win the title without losing a set. He was also a rare Champion in having no lady Champion to lead out for the first dance at the Wimbledon Ball. Instead, his wife, Wylita, had that honour.

The weather and erratic form played havoc with the Doubles seedings. Only Emerson and Santana (2) reached the quarter-finals unscathed and they went out in the semi-finals to France's Barclay and Darmon. Both the other semi-final pairs were unseeded, the Mexicans, Osuna and Palafox, coming through to win the title against the Frenchmen. This was the second Final between two unseeded pairs.

1964   In 1964 Fred Stolle (6) was seeded. The Committee would have been challenging fate to have left him out. Fred was determined that this would be his year and he more than justified his status by again getting to the Final. In the semi-final he had revenge over Chuck McKinley (2) 4/6, 10/8, 9/7, 6/4. Roy Emerson (1) reached his ordained Final place, suffering a 15/13 second set in his semi-final against Bungert, always an unseeded thruster.

A rain-interrupted Final saw a 12/10 second set which Emerson won to lead 2/0. Stolle rallied to take the third. But the swift-footed Emerson, who always seemed to carry too many big guns, won the fourth and the match to repeat his Australian Final win over Stolle, the eternal runner-up. Fred's day came at last when he won the French title next year and the American in 1966.

The Women's Championship saw the next encounter in the Billie Jean Moffitt–Margaret Smith saga, a saga which was to have many more enthralling and dramatic chapters. Billie Jean got to the semi-finals only after surviving shocks against Miss Beltrame of Italy whom she beat 7/5, 4/6, 6/3, and Margaret Lee, daughter of a British pre-war Davis Cup player, Harry Lee. In her semi-final against Billie Jean, Margaret Smith won the first set 6/3 and with a run of five games came from 4/1 behind in the second set to take the match.

In the Final she came up against Maria Bueno (2), a great Champion showing some signs of recapturing her old form. A classic was in prospect, presenting two big names and two contrasting styles. In the American championships of 1963, the first time they had met in an important Final, Maria Bueno had won 7/5, 6/4. In the recent French Championships Margaret Smith had triumphed 5/7, 6/1, 6/2.

A classic it proved to be, with jittery nerves showing raw edges to make a brilliant pattern cross-threaded with commonplace errors, forgivable only in the high tension and drama. Maria, all feline grace, took the first set 6/4 when, at the pinch, Margaret was again beset by Centre Court nerves. Margaret hit back in the second, winning four games in a row, but Maria squared at 4-all. The ninth was a very big game and full of fire and mettle, the advantage like a swinging pendulum. There were eight deuces and five break-points to Maria before Margaret at last hauled the game in. But it was only after sixteen exhausting games that she took the set 9/7.

At 3/3 in the third set came the final crisis of the match, and of the crowd's fever. Maria took Margaret's service for the loss of only one point and, the initiative seized, dropped just two more points in the next two games to win the match. Maria had regained her title and dethroned the reigning Champion to do so. The evenness of the struggle is shown by the fact that at match-point each player had won the same number of points throughout their duel. Maria took that match-point when a lucky bounce turned her despairing half-volley into an unreturnable drop-shot. After such a fine battle it was a cruel way for the guillotine to fall on the Champion.

Fred Stolle (2), who often gave the false impression of a wraith on court, was now armed anew with the French title, his first major singles' success. He tried hard but unsuccessfully in 1965 to lay his Wimbledon ghost. It was a case of third time plucky for stalwart Stolle, beaten again in the Final by his compatriot, Roy Emerson (1). This time Emerson won in straight sets. Stolle often suffered from being underestimated. Hopman said in 1963 that he was too old at twenty-five to play in the Davis Cup. But within a year he was helping Australia to win back the trophy from America.

Seldom can a player have felt so baffled by his Wimbledon bogey as Stolle. With Ken Rosewall and Gottfried von Cramm he shared rare records of frustration. Stolle equalled Von Cramm in reaching the Final three years running, but unlike him did it the first time unseeded. Stolle had to cope with Emerson twice and McKinley, whereas von Cramm was up against the major forces of Perry (twice) and Donald Budge, two of the candidates for the all-time top five. Furthermore, Von Cramm had fourteen years, during at least five of which he would have been at his best, denied him. Von Cramm had, with Rosewall and Gonzales, the best claim to be the greatest player who never won Wimbledon.

The year 1965 did not quite present the same Men's mixture as before. John Newcombe (6) was beginning to show himself as a thruster and failed only in the fourth round to Cliff Drysdale of South Africa, who won 9/7, 6/4, 11/13, 11/9. Lundquist (3), perhaps lucky to be seeded so high again, after early failures in previous years, was beaten by Allen Fox in the quarter-finals.

Having achieved semi-final eminence, Drysdale bowed out gracefully to Stolle. Drysdale was elegant in all he did. He even made two-handed strokes look polished.

Osuna (8) never lived up to the distinction of his 1963 American title, but he reached the quarter-finals and took the first set 13/11 from Stolle. Bungert (5) was comprehensively beaten in the third round by Marty Riessen, who was to prove a doughty competitor for years to come. Riessen, a typical American serve–volley merchant, was always difficult to beat, especially on fast grass courts, and to do so usually meant a long and exhausting encounter.

Tony Roche (7), in his third Wimbledon, fell to the soft guile of fellow Australian, Marty Mulligan. Roche, with his short, scything, left-handed service-swing, was regarded in the Australian camp as the natural successor to Laver. He certainly looked the part but, like Hoad some years before, he was dogged by injury, and in his case it happened before he reached the heights which his potential predicted.

South African, Keith Diepraam, reached the quarter-finals in Roche's place. He was also a big serve–volleyer and took the first set from Emerson. But after that first set he was a spent force and Emerson took three sets in a row. Diepraam had played Provincial cricket in South Africa and was a ferocious bowler – at least at the standard of the Wimbledon Press v. Players match, which takes place annually on the middle Sunday. George Worthington, that solid Australian player who became the very popular All England coach, was the unrelenting captain of the Players. He gloried in Diepraam's bouncers and the discomfort of the Press's batsmen.

In one of these matches came the ultimate in cricket history. The Australian No. 3 Test batsman, Bob Cowper, was caught by Okker at mid-on, from the bowling of Pietrangeli. 'White-flannelled fools' that they were, this was the first time that either had played cricket and the joy of this Dutch–Italian combination was such that you would have thought that they had just won the Wimbledon Doubles title. But this was won by Newcombe and Roche, the first of the five they have taken.

Maria Bueno (1) reached the semi-final of the Women's Singles where she met Billie Jean Moffitt (5). The two had clashed in the 1963 quarter-finals and then Billie Jean had won comfortably. This time Maria raced away to a 5/1 lead. The fighting Billie Jean pulled back the score to 4/5 but Maria served out to take the first set 6/4. Again in the second set the Champion broke first to lead 2/1, but this time Little Miss Moffitt started her rival earlier and with a run of four games went to 5/2 and on to take the set 7/5.

Into the deciding set and again Maria began well, twice breaking Billie Jean's service for a 4/1 lead. Billie Jean tried desperately to stem the flood and at 5/3 held off four match-points. But the fifth beat her and Maria was through to the Final.

Her opponent was Margaret Smith (2), who was in majestic form when

Take that! Cliff Drysdale makes even a two-handed shot elegant.

she beat Christine Truman in the semi-finals. And so the Final battle of the previous year was rejoined, but there was a difference. Margaret had for once conquered her Centre Court nerves. She played her usual commanding game, but this time it was not to be upset by jittery moments. Maria did establish an early 2/1 lead in the first set. However, Margaret, playing a powerful game which allowed little argument, swept to a 5/2 lead and took the set 6/4. In the second set a run of three games saw Maria take a 5/3 lead. Margaret pulled her back to square the set at 5/5 and then, controlling those disloyal nerves well, she held her service for 6/5 and took the Champion's to love.

So Margaret Smith grasped her second Wimbledon title and with it the third leg of the grand slam, which she completed when she won the American Championship at Forest Hills. This made her the first woman to win the world's four major titles, Australian, French, Wimbledon and American, in one year.

Her achievement was the reward for consistent effort. Of the three great tennis queens of recent years, Maria Bueno, Billie Jean King and Margaret, she was slightly below the other two as far as natural talent is concerned, but she has made up for this with dedication and application. She is a fine all-round athlete. She did weight-training to build up her arms, and running to develop her legs and stamina. She could have been an international sprinter. Her determination has always been fired by a fierce competitive spirit. Christine Truman, who played her often and knows her well, says of her: 'She did not let up for any day of the year and she just never seemed happy with herself unless she had played – and won – a game of tennis.'

It was the end of a Wimbledon era in women's tennis, an era in which Maria Bueno had mainly occupied the throne, with Margaret Smith a claimant come good. At her height, Maria had been a queen whose grace and power were without compare. Now a King would be Queen.

KING HIGH
1966–8

Billie Jean King has been one of the more controversial characters on the Wimbledon stage. Her record tells its own story – six times Champion, three times runner-up, four American titles, one Australian and one French. Moreover she won her titles in the second great era of women's tennis since 1946. Maria Bueno, though past her zenith, was still a Wimbledon Champion in 1964 after Little Miss Moffitt had made a considerable mark. Margaret Smith, the girl who really put women's tennis on the map in Australia and the winner of more major titles than any other player, was Billie Jean's main opponent in her heyday. Then, at the end of her reign she had to contend with the merciless precision of Chris Evert and the instinctive skill and ball-sense of Evonne Goolagong. Even so Billie Jean won her last title as recently as 1975.

On court she always had a love–hate relationship with the crowd. To begin with, spectators were intrigued by this tomboyish American with the Hussars' busby haircut, who chattered ferociously to herself as she came back to the baseline between points. They sensed in her a new giant, and new heroines are the lifeblood of spectator sports.

But then discord came into their feelings, as people saw in Billie Jean an apparent conceit rather than mere coltish cockiness. Now she was being pressured by her new double status, that of Champion and that of wife and breadwinner for her student husband. So whereas before she had wanted to win, now she *had* to. As far as spectators were concerned they were asking whether her extrovert mannerisms were to psyche herself – or her opponent.

Toughness in champions is essential and is normally applauded but it does not always sit prettily on a woman's countenance. Billie Jean has underlined her resolution in the way in which she has dedicated herself to what might be called a suffragette movement in women's tennis which, in a short time, has taken them to near parity in earning power with men. Her playing skills and the accelerating rewards of winning, made her the first woman athlete to earn over 100,000 dollars in one year from sport.

What made Billie Jean such a great Champion was not just the technical excellence of her American serve-volley game. Her seemingly unlimited determination made her above all a match-player rather than an exponent of her craft. And although she discarded her Hussars' busby hairstyle her court generalship increased. She hungered for victory and did everything possible to achieve it. Many Wimbledon spectators did not like what they felt to be her gamesmanship of upsetting the concentration of her opponents. What did opponents think of Billie Jean? Christine Truman, who often played and occasionally beat her, says: 'She definitely did not like losing but she took it all right. Off court she was very goodhearted and when I had my appendix out when I was in America she sent me flowers at the hospital.'

1966   The newly-wed Billie Jean brought her husband to the 1966 Wimbledon, where she was seeded four. Margaret Smith (1), the first woman grand slammer, looked in good enough form to retain her title, but as always there was the question mark against her of her Centre Court nerves. These showed in her opening set against Liz Starkie, which she won only 8/6. Margaret then sailed comfortably through to the semi-finals, where she came up against Billie Jean. At times Billie Jean had not looked too impressive in reaching the semi-finals. But like some great champions – particularly Hoad – she needed the stimulus of the big occasion or a crisis to bring out the best in her.

Against minor opponents she tended to give away more than did Maria Bueno and Margaret Smith. For example that year in the quarter-finals Billie Jean beat Annette van Zyl (6), 1/6, 6/2, 6/4. Annette not only won the first set but broke to lead 2/1 in the second, before Billie Jean took five games in a row. Again a little relaxation endangered her in the third set, when she lost her first two service games to be 3/0 down. Once more the crisis was met with a run of four winning games and the set and the match were soon won.

In the semi-final against the Champion, Billie Jean immediately put the pressure on Margaret's service and on her nerves. One forehand cross-court return of service and a backhand lob were executed with such command that the most confident opponent might have been shaken. Margaret lost that opening game and Billie Jean went on to win the set 6/3. Margaret rallied to take a 3/0 lead in the second set. Once again Billie Jean's match-play instinct rose to the occasion. She took the match by the throat and six successive games to win.

The other semi-final, between Maria Bueno (2) and Ann Jones (3), was a classical study in contrasts. Maria's game could be imperious or it could be fallible. The left-handed Ann was a steady, determined and persistent fighter. Her game, more suited to the clay of Paris's Roland Garros, had prevailed against Maria in the French semi-finals and Ann had gone on to win the French title for the second time.

In many ways it was surprising that Ann's lawn tennis was so defensive, for as a great table tennis player, who had reached the world title Final in 1957, she had possessed a fierce attacking forehand and it was table tennis which had inspired world champion Fred Perry's renowned forehand. Against Maria that day Ann had determined that her best chance lay in attack. Her

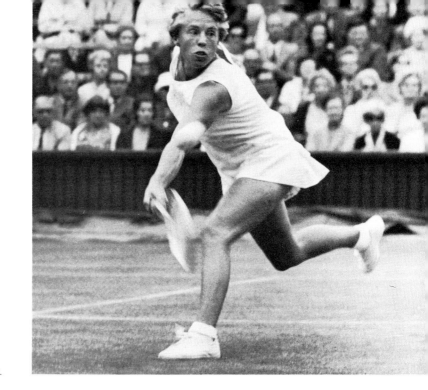

It shall not pass: Ann Jones,
Britain's best since the war.

Charlie Pasarell, speaking with
determined tongue.

backhand, normally a defensive chip, was played far more firmly and to a fuller length.

Maria took the first set 6/3 and led 3/1 in the second. Here Ann gritted her teeth and fought for every point, even for every stroke. She twice broke Maria's service and hung on and fought on, to take a gruelling second set 11/9, saving two match-points on the way.

Maria Bueno's answer was to win five games in a row at the start of the final set. Ann pulled back to 3/5, but when Maria got to 40–0 on her own service she seemed certain to take one of the three match-points. Ann saved them all, the third (the fifth of the match) with a stunning cross-court passing return of service which left Maria stranded.

The crowd was by now almost too tense to applaud, especially when in the next game Ann was 0–40 on her own service. Three more match-points to Maria. Again all of them were saved, and the set was square at 5/5. Maria went to 6/5 and then, with Ann serving, at 30–40, came the ninth match-point to the Brazilian. That, for Ann, was the fatal one. After two hours, during which spectators had been alternately on the edges of their seats and rising to their feet, Maria won a match which ranks as one of the most exciting in all Wimbledon's one hundred years.

Maria's Final with Billie Jean was a total contrast to her high-level match with Ann Jones. Maria reacted badly and made many mistakes, the first set going to Billie Jean 6/3 in seventeen minutes. Maria managed to win the second with imperious dismissal of her own imperfections, but when it mattered in the deciding third set, Billie Jean turned on full power, taking five games in a row, and came through with a long run to the winning post. Against this surge of power, Maria's game was again littered with errors. Afterwards, she declared that she had never played an important match so badly.

It was a horrible Wimbledon for weather – wet and cold for most of the fortnight. The conditions were almost certainly the cause of reigning Champion Roy Emerson failing to equal Fred Perry's achievement of winning the title in three successive years. Emerson (1), going for the hat-trick, was powerfully on course until in his quarter-final match with fellow countryman, left-hander Owen Davidson. Then, when chasing a wide ball at full speed (he was an international class sprinter) the slippery surface caused him to crash into the umpire's chair. He lay on the ground, his left shoulder hurt. He got up to carry on with the match, but with his movement restricted he lost.

Roy Emerson was not one of the great champions but he came very near to it. He was not as powerful as John Newcombe, whose star was now ascending, but each used his limited repertoire of strokes to maximum effect. Newcombe pulverized his opponents into submission, Emerson ground them down.

Roy's game, if it looked a bit mechanical, was efficiency itself and his greatest weapons were his fitness and speed of foot. He and McKinley were the outstanding men athletes of post-war years. His service, which was always dependable, had a flourishing wind-up all his own. He was neat to watch and very likeable, being unobtrusive and with perfect court manners. It was a mean stroke that fate played against him when he was in full flight for his third Championship.

Emerson's defeat let in Santana (4), who beat Davidson in five sets to reach the Final. Dennis Ralston (6) achieved the high status of Finalist in the lower half of the draw by beating Drysdale (7) in the semi-finals, the South African having surprisingly beaten Roche (2) in straight sets.

Neither Santana nor Ralston had been in the Final before. Once again the crowd were able to look forward to a fascinating clash of styles, the touch artistry of Santana against the thundering power of Ralston. Artistry emerged triumphant and Santana won 6/4, 11/9, 6/4. It was artistry allied to determination. In the second set Santana was 4/1 down. He came back to 5/6, but still Ralston was serving for the set. This crucial game was the longest of the match and went to five deuces and it was Santana who won it and eventually the set and match.

The Spaniard will go down in the memories and hearts of tennis enthusiasts as one of the most delightful players to watch for his toreador grace and ease of stroke, both heightened by his superb anticipation. In Spain he became a national hero, rivalling top matadors and top footballers. After winning Wimbledon, he was awarded the high national honour of the Cross of Isabel la Catolica. His birthplace, Madrid, awarded him the Gold Medal of the city.

Santana was a tennis wizard. His racket was a conjuror's wand, with which he would disguise the intended direction of a shot. He could use top-spin on backhand or forehand, so that the ball dipped maddeningly at his opponent's feet or cleared him with a perfect lob that raced tauntingly on, uncatchable. And he could slice and chop with such spin that the ball seemed to hang in the air. He would admit to having a little temperament and getting mad with himself. But he was a most likeable and modest man with the broadest of smiles ('I smile a lot because I love tennis for itself and for what it has done for me'). When congratulated after winning the title he said: 'Emerson is the real winner.'

67   Within a year, Santana's sporting approach was having to survive a tougher test. Opening on the Centre Court, as is the Champion's right on the first day, he was beaten in the first round of the 1967 Championship by Charlie Pasarell. Pasarell had already established himself as a most difficult customer for any player at any stage of the Championship. In that opening round Santana found the drizzle, which occurred at times during the match, restricted the footwork which was the basis of his touch shots. Pasarell fell several times but refused to be inhibited and maintained his all-out attacking style. In the deciding fourth set at 6/6 he hit four clean forehand winners to break Santana's service and then held his own to love for the match. It was the first time that

the Champion and for that matter the No. 1 seed had been beaten in the first round.

The match between Bungert and Wilson was a highlight. Bungert played with the ramrod back of a Prussian guardsman and the wrist of a swordsman. His touch was delicate and his game inspired. When two players of this calibre are both hitting top form each raises the other's game. So the spectators were treated to fine rally after fine rally, full of dazzling strokes and exquisite ploys. The finesses, the wrong-footing, the whispered drop-shots had the crowd applauding and purring. Wilson's flair fired brightly and quickly and he won the first set 6/1 and the second 7/5. Bungert took the third and fourth 6/1, 7/5 and had just that much more strength in reserve to win the final set 9/7, at the end putting Wilson to the sword with fierce forehand winners.

In the semi-final Bungert dashed further British hopes when he beat Roger Taylor in a tough five-set battle. This made him the fifth unseeded player to reach the Final. When Roy Emerson (2) succumbed to the big serve and sharp volleying of Nikki Pilic, it meant that of the semi-finalists only John Newcombe (3) had a seed to his name. He exerted his authority by first out-hitting Pilic and then in the Final overwhelming a disappointing Bungert. None could deny, however, the compelling way in which Newcombe settled his account to win the title. It was a masterful progress. The Doubles title saw the names Hewitt and McMillan (2) inscribed for the first time on the Roll of Honour.

The field in the Women's Singles was weakened by the absence of Margaret Smith. Billie Jean King (1) blitzed through to the Final, beating on the way Virginia Wade (8), seeded for the first time. Maria Bueno (2) went out in the fourth round to little but lively Rosie Casals. Having disposed of Maria, Rosie, who looked like a gym-slipped schoolgirl, beat Judy Tegart to meet Ann Jones (3) for the second successive year, this time for a place in the Final.

Rosie, with her all-court game functioning well, began with a precocious burst, winning the first set in twenty minutes 6/2. She seemed unstoppable, playing every kind of shot, and all of them coming off. But Ann Jones is not one to be swept aside that easily, or at all. She kept her nerve, saw that for her to stand a chance the pace of the match had to be changed, and so set about waging a war of attrition. At Ann's nagging dictate the rallies began to lengthen and suddenly Rosie was no longer dominating the game. Ann pursued the wearing-down process until the very end, by which time, having hit many fine passing shots past the at times bewildered Rosie, Ann had won by two sets to one.

So at her twelfth Wimbledon challenge, and after being five times a semi-finalist, Ann Jones got to the Final. The main difference in that Final between Ann and Billie Jean King was the way in which they played the big points. Here the Champion's match temperament shone through. In the opening game

Newcombe and Roche on the way to the first of their five Wimbledon Doubles titles, 1965.

Made Safe. Hewitt and McMillan (*left*) take the second of their two titles, against Smith and Van Dillen, 1972.

for example Billie Jean needed to save three break-points. She did so and then followed by capturing Ann's service.

But Ann could look back with satisfaction on a year which not only brought her her first Final but which signalled her as a better player, particularly on the backhand which was no longer purely defensive. This new-look Ann Jones confirmed the strengthened belief in herself by reaching the Final of the American Championships at Forest Hills later that year, where she again lost to Billie Jean, whose belief in herself already seemed total. Billie Jean completed the triple crown with Rosie Casals in the Women's Doubles and with Owen Davidson in the Mixed. This was the first triple crown since Frank Sedgman's in 1952 and the first women's since Doris Hart's in 1951.

The All England Club, a sanctuary of tradition, has always been ready to create new ones and to experiment. So it was not altogether surprising when, with the war of words, resolutions and attitudes over the question of Open tennis at its height and seemingly unending, the far-sighted Chairman Herman David (who back in 1935 had advocated Open tennis) and the Committee took the initiative. In August 1967 Wimbledon opened its Doherty Gates to professionals and staged an all-professional tournament. This was the first and probably the last as, spurred on by Britain, other countries accepted the principle of Open tournaments and the following year the Wimbledon Championships were open to amateurs and professionals alike.

That pioneering first all-professional event saw the return to Wimbledon of previous amateur giants and favourites like Hoad, Gonzales and Rosewall. It was won by one of the most recent favourites and great champions of all – Rod Laver.

1968   The crowds flocked joyously to Wimbledon for the return of Laver and company for the 1968 Championships. For over the last few years the Women's Championship had contained more star names than the Men's. Some of the professionals themselves were a shade apprehensive about their return. Their fears were founded on a shortage of real five-set championship play in the professional ranks and the lack of variety in the opposition they met. These fears had been underscored by events at the British Hard Courts Championship at Bournemouth that year – the first Open tournament in the world. There, Mark Cox had beaten Pancho Gonzales in a five-set second round match and then put out Roy Emerson in straight sets in the quarter-finals. Laver had put a stop to the rot and salvaged professional pride when he won the title, but doubts remained.

The weather at Wimbledon that year was capricious and, for the first few days, downright appalling, which of course produced smaller gates. Because of the mixed amateur/professional entry with in many cases little previous comparative form, sixteen men were seeded for the first time since the experiment of 1950. How glorious it was to see the mighty Hoad again and Gonzales and Rosewall and all the top names in tennis. Wimbledon was revitalized. It

Rod Laver: dead reckoning.

No crossed fingers for Billie Jean
Moffitt (Mrs King).

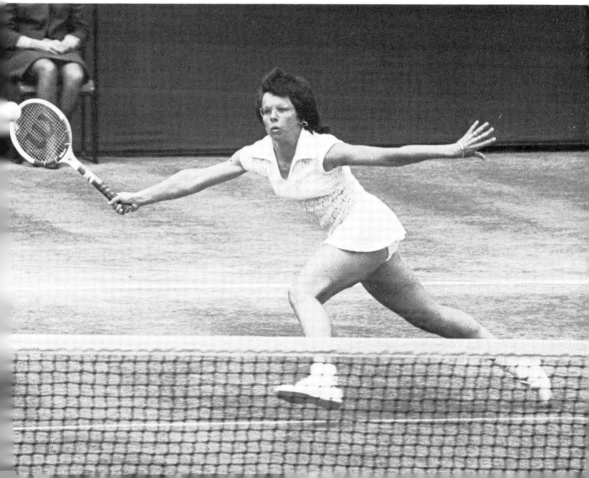

had never lost its position of being the world's pre-eminent tournament. Now greatness had returned.

The professional career of Hoad (10) had been a short one, brought to an early end by persistent back trouble and with his wife Jenny he had started a tennis ranch in Spain. There were enough reminders of his once all-conquering power to bring back memories and it took the deftness, resilience and good service return of Bob Hewitt to beat him in five sets in the third round. Gonzales (8) reached the same barrier where Alex Metreveli of Russia beat him in four.

Rod Laver (1) was still the outstanding professional player, so that his number one seeding was unquestionable. Compared to his 1962 performance, when he dropped only one set to Santana, his results made him seem more vulnerable. He lost a set in the first round to Eugene Scott, one to Riessen in the third and another to Cox in the fourth. In the quarter-finals he dropped two sets to Ralston (9). But hoeing this hard row had honed his game into top shape. In the semi-finals he showed masterful form to beat Arthur Ashe (13) 7/5, 6/2, 6/4.

So Laver got to the Final, where Rosewall (2) was seeded to meet him in what everybody hoped would be the Final to end all Finals and so mark this important year. Alas for hopes and Ken's many admirers, for in the fourth round he went down to the big serve of left-hander Tony Roche (15). Roche went on to dispose of big-game specialists Buchholz (10) and Graebner to meet Laver in the second left-handers' final. In it Roche showed his power, but Laver had more and could control it to play any shot. It took him sixty-seven minutes to win his third title.

Although other famous names had looked vulnerable and some had fallen before they should, Laver had never looked a loser. His dominance had not always been obvious but, aware of the demands of seven rounds of possibly five sets each, he paced himself with rare judgement and his play always had the mark of authority. He was truly now world champion. Newcombe and Roche could consider themselves so, too, for they won the Doubles for the second time.

Billie Jean King (1), who with Ann Jones (4) had turned professional in 1967, maintained her position as Wimbledon queen. She had to fight in the semi-final against long-standing rival Ann, but Billie Jean never minded a fight. Ann took the first set 6/4 and went to a 5/3 lead in the second. Then Billie Jean, raising her game to the heights to meet the crisis, got back on level terms and was never headed again.

Billie Jean's final opponent was Judy Tegart (7), surprise winner over Margaret Court (2), now married after a year away. After a testing struggle Billie Jean beat Judy 9/7, 7/5. With her extrovert good humour Judy was a great favourite of the crowd. She was also a doughty fighter and came back strongly after losing the first three games of the match. Once again Billie Jean showed that when it was most needed, her temperament had a finer edge and she could find the right shot in her locker. At 4/4 in the second set she was 30–40. She saved the break-point with a forehand volley down the line which left her opponent helpless.

King was still Queen and riding high.

12

TWILIGHT OF THE
GODS *1969–72*

1969   In 1969, Rod Laver (1) marked himself down as a candidate for the title of the greatest player of all time and certainly proved that he was the supreme player of the decade when he retained his Wimbledon title.

Laver's progress was punctuated by moments when certainty was not always apparent. In the second round, for instance, against India's Premjit Lall he lost the first two sets. Lall won three games in the third set but was not permitted to win any in the fourth and fifth. In the semi-final Rod met the rising star Arthur Ashe (5) and the two of them combined to put on a breathtaking display of searing pace – so fluently controlled. In the Final, Rod dropped a set to John Newcombe (6) but he never looked like losing.

What an outstanding Champion he was. He has come to Wimbledon ten times, won the title on four of them and in two of the other six was a losing Finalist. The fact that he came back and won again after a five-year absence, with all his main rivals in the field, suggests that he could have won eight times to beat the record of Willie Renshaw – and in a much tougher competitive era. In this year he won the title at the five major meetings in which he competed. This gave him his second grand slam. Only one other player had even done it once.

Greatness, in the vintage year of 1969, was not confined to Laver. It was revealed as early as the first round. Pancho Gonzales (12) was drawn against Charlie Pasarell, who two years before had written himself into the record books when he beat Santana and became the first player to oust the reigning Champion in the first round.

The Gonzales–Pasarell match, for all who experienced it, transcended anything that had gone before. It was longer and more dramatic even than the legendary Drobny–Patty marathon of 1953. That had lasted ninety-three games and four hours twenty minutes. This ended only after 112 games and five hours twelve minutes of broken time, broken temper and finally broken spirit. It was a match of heroic proportions which belonged in soul to an earlier age, when it would have come down in song and mime and have passed into folklore.

Gonzales, serving second, was struggling from behind throughout the first set. He had set-point against him at 12/13, two more at 14/15, two more at 17/18 and a further three at 20/21. Altogether Pasarell failed to clinch eleven

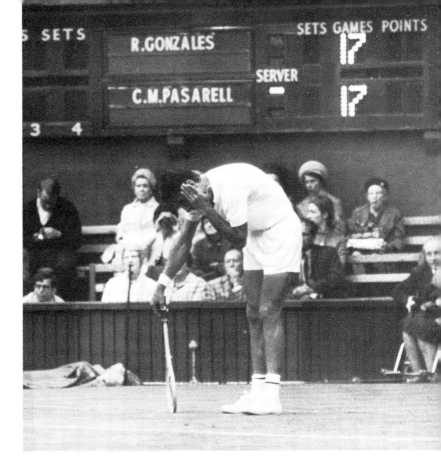

A hard day's night for Gonzales, 1969. He finally won 22/24, 1/6, 16/14, 6/3, 11/9.

Alarm ball for Rosie Casals.

set-points in that record-equalling set of forty-six games. At last he got home on the twelfth.

The light was already poor and the umpire would certainly have called the players in at Lord's. Gonzales appealed. The umpire telephoned the Referee for a ruling. The answer was 'play on'. Gonzales did not take it with good grace and at forty-one he could not be blamed. He so far forgot his pro-fessionalism as to make scarcely more than a pretence of playing and lost the second set 6/1. His gesticulations to the umpire and to the Referee, who was now on the sidelines, brought boos from the crowd. At last, after two hours and twenty minutes the Referee, Captain Gibson, called it a day. Gonzales stalked off in fury, the whites of his eyes gleaming against his swarthy face and the gathering gloom.

The match was resumed the next day at 2.42. It seemed unlikely that, after the stresses of the previous evening, grandfather Gonzales could give fifteen years to as tough a character as Charlie Pasarell. But, having gone away in dudgeon the night before, Gonzales had returned full of consuming purpose. This was evident from his whole bearing and from every shot he played. For it was Gonzales who was always putting the pressure on Pasarell. The games mounted. So did the set-points, two at 6/5, four more at 11/10, the seventh at 14/13 and the eighth at 15/14 when Pasarell, having served a double-fault, could win only one more point. The set had lasted an hour and twenty-eight minutes.

The fourth set was in minor key. Pasarell had one point to break service but could not take it, whereas at 3/4 and 30–40 he double-faulted. The set was there for Gonzales to take and he served out to 15. The match had now lasted four hours sixteen minutes with the overnight break. No match had received more coverage nor aroused more feeling than this conflict of such un-parallelled magnitude. Where Gonzales had been booed off court the night before by a slightly misunderstanding crowd, today they cheered and cheered him on.

The final set provided a fitting climax to even what had gone before. All those present at the drama's dénouement sensed the prize at risk – the huge pride of this truly great player – Gonzales. Pasarell went to 5/4 and suddenly, after the hours of struggle Gonzales was 0–40. It seemed that only a thunder-bolt from Jove could save him. After Pasarell had lobbed out to lose the first match-point, the thunderbolt came through a Gonzales service which crash-saved the second and Pasarell lost the third when he failed with another lob.

At 5/6, Gonzales was again in a morass of trouble at 0–40. All three match-points were tossed aside – with a smash, a glancing forehand volley and yet another cannonball serve. If hearts had been thumping earlier, they were now at danger level. 6/6, 7/7, 7/8 and Gonzales, after two deuces, had the seventh match-point against him. Again Pasarell tried the lob. Again it went out.

9/9 and at last Pasarell was spent. He lost his service to love and Gonzales went out to love on his own.

The final score was 22/24, 1/6, 16/14, 6/3, 11/9 – 112 games. An exhausted BBC radio commentator returned listeners to the studio with, 'That's all – believe me *all* – from Wimbledon.'

The euphoria made the crowds feel that Gonzales was almost superhuman, that nothing was beyond him and that even at forty-one he could win the title, for which he had been the favourite twenty years before. He won two more rounds comfortably enough, but then in the fourth round went out to Arthur Ashe.

What a superlative champion Gonzales could have been. This Colossus, who bestrode the Centre Court with such magnificence, was never seen at Wimbledon when at his best, having turned professional at twenty-one in 1949. Just before that he had made his one Wimbledon appearance as an amateur, when as No. 2 seed he was beaten by Geoff Brown in the fourth round, but he had won the Doubles title with Frankie Parker. His best years were in the professional ranks where for nine years between 1951 and 1960 he was the world No. 1.

He was born in California of Mexican parents. In the back streets around his home tennis was regarded as a cissy game and young Ric's most burning ambition was to own a bicycle. Instead, when he was twelve, his mother bought him a loosely-strung tennis racket. At first it was scorned, but after one game it became treasured. He took it to bed. He talked to it. Every morning he would get up at three o'clock to do a paper round to pay for balls and court fees. He played truant from school once too often and his angry father broke the precious racket over his knee.

Ann Jones (4) had not had to follow quite that path, but she kept up her resolve and determination over years of getting to within reach of the title but without managing to grasp it. Her victory in 1969 came at her thirteenth attempt after being five times a semi-finalist and once getting to the Final. On the clay courts of Stade Roland Garros, more suited to her game, she had twice won the French title. To win Wimbledon, Ann had to account for two of the all-time greats of women's tennis. In the semi-final she beat Margaret Court (1) 10/12, 6/3, 6/2. In this match she again showed the new style, revealed the previous year, when she gave Billie Jean King such a fight in the semi-final. Having lost the first set against the powerful Australian, Ann moved onto the attack and outplayed her opponent.

In the Final Ann was again a set down to Billie Jean, but again she grew in strength to win 3/6, 6/3, 6/2. This was the culmination of her tennis career. There was no shrewder tactician than Ann Jones. Year by year she had attacked the inner citadel, always seeking to strengthen her weapons, and had finally captured it at her thirteenth attempt.

Ken Rosewall was a hero of different proportions to Gonzales. His immaculate tennis and demeanour had long made him a Wimbledon favourite. This had been enhanced by his 'little boy lost' look when he turned with drooping shoulder and seemingly reluctant step back to the baseline, pulling at an eyelash and apparently about to burst into tears. He looked like this so often that those who knew him were not deceived. It was merely Ken concentrating.

In the 1954 Final he had been beaten by Drobny. He and Hoad had played a memorable Final in 1956, after which Ken had turned professional. On his return with the professionals, for the first Open in 1968, Tony Roche had shut the gate on him, while the following year he had fallen unexpectedly to Bob Lutz. As far as Wimbledon titles were concerned he had been written off. But he had other ideas.

Rod Laver came to the 1970 Wimbledon, aiming to complete a hat-trick of successes. There seemed to be no reason why he should not but his hopes were ended by Roger Taylor (16) when, in a fourth round battle of left-handers, Taylor won in four sets. Roger had never played better and, on a day when the temperature touched ninety, it was Laver who wilted under the pressure. It was his last challenge but one before the centenary year.

Taylor, in a battle of the big servers, then beat Clark Graebner (9) 6/3, 11/9, 12/10 to reach his second semi-final. His Yorkshire resolution and fighting quality had brought him a long way but he went down now to the perennial skills of Ken Rosewall, who beat him 6/3, 4/6, 6/3, 6/3 and earned his third bite at the Champion's cherry.

In the Final Rosewall met big John Newcombe (2), who had been using his bludgeoning serve–volley game to powerful effect. Rosewall saved a set-point at 4/5 and, capturing Newcombe's service, went out 7/5 on his own. Newcombe took the second set 6/3 to square the match and with a run of five games took the third to lead 2 sets to 1. Back came the ageless 'Little Master' in the fourth set with a run of five games to make it two sets all. Now though, he was spent and his familiar dejected look this time reflected reality. At 1/1 in the final set Newcombe started another run of five games to win the match. Rosewall was given a lasting ovation, partly because spectators felt they were saying goodbye to such an old favourite, who must surely realize that he could not 'come again'. But Ken still had another surprise up his short sleeve.

In 1970, both Billie Jean (1) and Margaret Court (2) were back and both got through to the Final. They produced the match of the Championship – certainly the best women's match since the war. Both players were at their peak, both utterly determined to regain the title. Nearly every rally was a minor masterpiece. Up to 8-all in the 14/12 first set (won by Margaret Court), half the games went against the server, and this in a match involving two of the most effective serves in women's tennis.

In the first half of that set there were twenty-two deuces and eighteen break-points, eight against Billie Jean and ten against Margaret. In the second half there were no deuces until the twelfth and thirteenth games. There were five

Hoad and Rosewall. Muscles
ageing...

...ageless Muscles.

break-points and two set-points. The twenty-six games of the set made it the longest played in a Wimbledon singles Final by men or women.

The second set, though shorter, was even more pulsating. At 7/6, Margaret Court had match-point which Billie Jean saved with a forehand volley down the line which even Margaret could not reach. In the next game Billie Jean had two break-points, but could not convert them. It was 8/8, 9/9, 10/9, with Margaret Court leading. Suddenly Billie Jean, at 15–40, faced her second match-point.

That final game alone was worth the admission money. From 15–40 Billie Jean drew on the dregs of her stamina and spirit to play like a demon. She saved four match-points. The fifth (the sixth in all) was too much and settled the issue of this superb duel. Margaret Court had won 14/12, 11/9, forty-six games played over two hours twenty-six minutes, beating the previous record of forty-four games set in 1919 in the famous Challenge Round between Suzanne Lenglen and Mrs Lambert Chambers.

Margaret Court's triumph was all the more incredible as she had been suffering from a tendon injury in her ankle and had been given pain-killing injections both for her semi-final and for the Final. Perhaps the ultimate spur to her fight was the knowledge that this might be her last chance to win the grand slam. This she achieved at Forest Hills a few weeks later, to equal the record of Maureen Connolly.

In the aftermath of that fantastic Final few people took much notice of the arrival and the first round dismissal of an eighteen-year-old Australian girl. Her coach, Vic Edwards, said, 'By 1973 she could win Wimbledon' but for most the girl came to mind only because of her strange name – Evonne Goolagong.

1971   The following year Evonne was to bring a breath of fresh Antipodean air to the Centre Court. Evonne's grandfather is an aborigine and her name means 'tall trees by still water'. She entirely lives up to the onomatopoeia of her name. Her game is happy grace, as instinctive and natural as a gazelle. She had three apparent weaknesses in an otherwise complete game, her forehand was sliced and could break down, her second service was soft and inclined to be short and, every now and then she appeared 'to go walk-about' as the media soon dubbed it. When she did, a flawless performance could fall to pieces. She would continue to play through her part while her mind and spirit were evidently elsewhere.

Still just nineteen, but already heralded as the new French champion, Evonne was seeded 3 to Billie Jean King (2) and Champion Margaret Court (1). She got through to the semi-finals, there to be confronted with the re-doubtable Billie Jean. She started by taking on the former Champion at her own serve–volley game. Strangely Billie Jean's play lacked its usual bite and accuracy and Evonne won the first set 6/4. She became slightly more defensive in the second set but managed to remain in command to win that and the match.

Smash and grab artists:
ABOVE 1972: Newcombe takes Smith.
ABOVE RIGHT 1973: Smith's turn...as 'Nasty'
covers up RIGHT

In the quarter-finals Margaret Court had beaten Winnie Shaw, the only Briton to get as far, which she did unseeded. This sunny Scot played a most attractive game. In her semi-final Margaret met fellow Australian Judy Dalton, dropped the first set but then allowed her opponent to take only one more game. It must have been of particular satisfaction to Margaret to see Australian girls taking three of the four semi-final places, as it had been her own amazing record which had been largely responsible for the surge in women's tennis interest in Australia.

In the Final Margaret soon showed her Centre Court nerves by losing the first four games. She rallied to win three games but Evonne held her off like a veteran to take the set 6/4. In the second set Evonne took five games running to lead 5/1 and 0–40 on Margaret's service. Margaret found the desperate courage of the mortally wounded to save three match-points but lost a fourth when nerves twitched at her serving arm for a double-fault. Evonne Goolagong had done it two years before Vic Edwards had said she might.

Rod Laver (1) was again the top men's seed with reigning Champion John Newcombe (2). Newcombe justified his selection by winning a five-set Final against Stan Smith (4) to take his third Singles title. He will go down as a rugged champion, whose fighting spirit always enabled him to make the best of his talents.

Ken Rosewall (3) did not let his fans down. He played the match of the tournament in the quarter-finals against American Cliff Richey (6), coming back from 6/8, 5/7 to win the last three sets 6/4, 9/7, 7/5. The match started at 3.30 and lasted a minute under four hours. It was another tremendous performance by the 'Little Master' but Rosewall then suffered reaction and fell easily to his 1970 Final conqueror, Newcombe. Laver again went down in the quarter-finals, this time to American Tom Gorman.

This year saw the first use at Wimbledon of the tie-break. Many had thought that this device, brought in to shorten matches, would never come to Wimbledon. But with true British compromise it was used at eight all and not six all as in the rest of the world, the final set remaining an advantage one.

1972   In 1972, Billie Jean King (2) was intent on re-establishing her authority. Virginia Wade was also making a strong bid and had won the Australian title, beating Evonne Goolagong in the Final. In the French Championship Evonne again got to the Final, but there Billie Jean beat her.

So to Wimbledon. Evonne (1) got the top seed as reigning Champion. If the seeding ran true to form she was due to meet the new American sensation, Chrissie Evert (4), in the semi-finals. A year before, at only sixteen (even younger than Maureen Connolly when she first played Wightman Cup), Chrissie had been the main instrument in America winning that trophy and, with her relentless precision and attacking double-fisted backhand, had won forty-six consecutive singles before Billie Jean ended her precocious run in the US semi-finals. She had become the youngest player to reach that stage.

Evonne Goolagong, 1971
Champion, in the mood.

Chrissie Evert – a champion
crystallized.

The tennis world awaited the Evert–Goolagong clash, for somehow these two rising stars had not as yet played each other. As the girls came out onto court to a tremendous welcome, seventeen-year-old Chrissie, her remarkable composure already a byword, appeared the senior to the twenty-year-old Champion. Both were beautifully dressed and looked delightful as they turned to make the traditional bow to the Royal Box. Evonne had already established her place in the crowd's affections. Chrissie, on the other hand, was immaculate not only in her dress, but also in the almost mechanical perfection of her length and accuracy. So many felt that she was cold and they responded to her as they did between the wars to Helen Wills. But the next year or two brought Chrissie almost as much affection and admiration as Evonne.

The match began with both playing tentatively, as though taking each other's measure, and the two opening service games were lost. Gradually Chrissie gained slight ascendancy. It was a fascinating duel, with purity of stroke predominating. Chrissie's drives, particularly on the two-handed side, got ever nearer the lines. Her accuracy was a revelation. She took the first set after thirty-four enthralling minutes.

When Chrissie went to 3/0 in the second set it began to look as if Billie Jean's prediction would be fulfilled. She had said: 'I think Chrissie is the more mature. She is stronger mentally. She has basically only three or four shots and there is less to go wrong with her game.' But then it was as if pride had pricked Evonne with a spur. She struck an irresistible vein. Seven games in a row gave her the set 6/3 and 1/0 in the final set. Thrust and counter-thrust, with breathtaking shots by both girls took Evonne to 5/4. With Chrissie serving, Evonne prepared the *coup de grâce*, with two superb shots, a backhand drop-volley for 0–15, and a chopped forehand cross-court passing shot for 0–30. She finished the game to love and with it the match.

It had been an hour and thirty-three minutes of sheer tennis delight, promising still more riches when these two candidates for all-time greatness met in the future. The crowd gave them a standing ovation.

This was 1972 Wimbledon's finest hour. Evonne was so popular and yet so unspoilt. Alf Chave, a Queenslander who came over yearly to be a brilliant summarizer for BBC Radio, was staying with Vic Edwards during the fortnight. He told how Evonne, away from Wimbledon, was leading the ordinary life of a young girl. While weaving her way in glory through the Wimbledon draw, she was still doing her share of the washing-up and other chores, though she had been allowed one excursion to nearby Putney to buy herself a dress for the Wimbledon Ball.

Evonne was now through to the Final against Billie Jean, who on the way had put out Virginia Wade (7) in the quarter-finals. Billie Jean won the Final 6/3, 6/3, with a performance which recalled her dominance of earlier years. After knee operations, she herself said that she was back to full fitness and form, 'I could run and bend the way I did in 1966.' Once again she was queen.

Internecine quarrels between WCT and the ILTF had the effect of barring from this Wimbledon four of the leading players who had contracts with World Championship Tennis – Rod Laver, Ken Rosewall, Arthur Ashe and reigning Champion, John Newcombe. It was particularly sad that Big John was denied the chance of going for his hat-trick. He tried. He submitted a private entry but the management committee regretfully had to turn him down, since the ILTF had ruled that contract professionals must be barred.

In their absence, Stan Smith, the previous year's Finalist and current American Champion, was the natural No. 1 seed. Nastase was No. 2. They met in the Final – postponed for twenty-four hours due to rain and the first match ever played at Wimbledon on a Sunday. Stan Smith, blond, handsome and 6 feet 4 inches with his straight-backed walk, might well have stepped out of Sandhurst with the Sword of Honour. He was in fact a serving member of the US Army, had been in the American top ten since 1966 and was now the established No. 1. His was the big serve and volley game and, with his reach, he could command the net and was extremely difficult to lob.

Smith looked an officer but was in fact doing his draft service in the ranks. Nastase, though not of conventional military appearance, said with typical impish humour before the match, 'I *am* an officer.' He admitted that he was nervous after the day's postponement in a rain-bedevilled Wimbledon, but said with a typical shrug, 'I will fight Godzilla' – a Rumanian horror film monster, whom he jokingly likened to Smith.

Nastase is a tennis genius and his deft but wayward style totally contrasted with the orthodox Smith. In a match which proved to be one of Wimbledon's most exciting finals, Nastase got the first edge and the first set 6/4. The twenty-four-hours delay had generated a lot of nervous tension which sparked off incredible service returns and brilliant rallies in the second set, which Smith took 6/3. It had been noticeable that 'Nasty', who had been behaving beautifully, was getting edgy – changing rackets often and showing other signs of temperament. This inevitably affected his own inspiration and Smith romped away with the third set to lead 2/1 and then 1/0 in the fourth. Nastase changed rackets yet again, found his touch and won the fourth set 6/4 to square the match.

All this had scarcely been Sunday-afternoon-on-the-vicarage-lawn tennis and the crowd delighted in the searing drives, the touch volleys, deceptive passing shots, the exquisite lobs and the thundering smashes. The final set provided a fitting climax. At 2/2 Smith was three times break-point down and held on only after seven deuces. At 4/4 Smith was 0–30. Nastase hit a forehand volley hard and true. Smith, with a mighty Godzilla leap of desperation, just reached the ball with the frame of his racket. It dropped dead – on the other side of the net. Had that shot failed Nastase must surely have won the title.

In the next game Nastase had to fend off two match-points. Again, at 5/6 down, he faced match-point and saved it with a forehand volley which defied even Smith's telescopic reach. A forehand volley gave Smith match-point again and he rammed it home for the title. The match had lasted two hours forty-four minutes and was classed by many as the best Men's Final since the Crawford–Vines epic in 1933.

13

CONNORS ASKS THE
QUESTIONS 1973–6

No sooner had one ugly political argument been settled than another was raised. As a result of Nikki Pilic being suspended by the ILTF for failing to play in a Davis Cup match, and his consequent barring from Wimbledon, the Association of Tennis Professionals called upon all its members to withdraw their entries. The arguments swung to and fro, always with the underlying feeling that nobody could do such a thing to Wimbledon. A formula would surely be found.

In the end, principle prevailed and seventy-nine players, including thirteen of the sixteen seeds, withdrew. There were three exceptions, two of them especially notable: Roger Taylor, with pressures from both sides, came down for Yorkshire and All England and overnight became still more a hero. With him as a strange pedestal-fellow was Ilie Nastase, a rebel and quixotic as one might expect.

The immediate effect was a surge of loyalty from the fans. Whenever Roger Taylor appeared he was cheered rapturously. Nastase (1) was given top place in the re-seeding with Kodes of Czechoslovakia (not a member of ATP) at 2, Taylor (3), Alex Metreveli of Russia (4) and Jimmy Connors (5). At No. 6 was a newcomer but with a reputation which had preceded him – straight from Valhalla it seemed – seventeen-year-old Bjorn Borg of Sweden. Squealing and screaming teenage girls followed his progress in droves. Never before has such a posse of policemen been needed to protect a player.

Nastase should have had a great chance for the title, but in the fourth round a newcomer, Alex 'Sandy' Mayer of the USA, beat him in four sets. Mayer went on to the semi-finals where he met Metreveli, whose all-round but unforceful game had contained the up-and-coming Jimmy Connors. Metreveli won the semi-final to become the first Russian to get to the Wimbledon Singles Final.

The other semi-final featured Roger Taylor as star billing. In a stirring five-set quarter-final he had dealt with that other precocious youngster, Borg. Taylor's semi-final opponent was Jan Kodes. Taylor, with his big serve game well in tune, had been showing his best form, and seemed to have a fine chance to take the title. He gave the semi-final all he had got, but it was Kodes who emerged the winner 8/9, 9/7, 5/7, 6/4, 7/5. Once there, the Czech's experience proved too much for a slightly overawed Metreveli and Kodes won 6/1, 9/8, 6/3. Connors got his first title and Nastase some consolation when they

Left to right: Virginia Wade; Evonne Goolagong (Mrs Cawley); Ted Tinling; Rosie Casals; Billie Jean King.

1973: ATP withdraws its players.
Alex Metreveli, the first Russian in
the Men's Finals...

...but the first Czech ever, Jan
Kodes, skis his chance.

teamed up (1) to win the Doubles. But the biggest triumph belonged to Wimbledon – triumph of spirit over circumstance.

While Borg and Connors had been giving notice to their elders that a new order was on the way, in the Women's Championship Chris Evert was again straining at the leash, putting out Margaret Court (1) 6/1, 1/6, 6/1 in the semi-finals. In the Final Chrissie came up against the indomitable Billie Jean King (2), who again had fought off the challenge of Evonne Goolagong. Billie Jean clearly set out to repeat the lesson she had taught her young compatriot in the Forest Hills semi-final two years before. She took the first set in sixteen minutes, allowing her opponent just nine points. In the second set things started to look even worse for Chrissie. Billie Jean took the first two games for the loss of only one point.

Chrissie did not despair. She became Evert unremitting, and was rewarded. At 1/3 she took three games in a row and it was suddenly noticeable that Billie Jean had become uncertain. But yet again, when it was most needed, the Champion raised her game and at 5/5 broke service and held her own for the match and her fifth Singles title – a remarkable achievement. Billie Jean completed a clean sweep to gain her second triple crown.

1974 Billie Jean's (1) record-chasing was brought to a summary halt in the 1974 Women's Singles with quarter-final defeat by Olga Morozova (8), 7/5, 6/2. The popular and athletic Olga continued by beating Virginia Wade (5) 1/6, 7/5, 6/4 in the semi-finals, to follow in the steps of Alex Metreveli and become the first Russian woman to reach a Wimbledon Final. There she was to meet Chrissie Evert (2).

To get there Chrissie had survived a first round marathon against Australian Lesley Hunt 8/6, 5/7, 11/9 – the forty-six games equalling the length of the King–Court final of 1970. In the Final her relentless accuracy was too much for Olga Morozova. The Russian fought valiantly in the opening game which went to five deuces but Chrissie won and went on to take the set 6/0. In the second, Olga led 2/1, was pulled back to 2/4, recovered to 4/4 but Evert broke again and won the set and match 6/4.

In both the Men's and Women's Championships, the younger players were thrusting forward while the seasoned campaigners fought to hold off the challenge. In the thick of the battle there was still evergreen Ken Rosewall (9). In 1974 he beat successively Barry Phillips, Moore, Vijay Amritraj, Kanderal of Switzerland, Roscoe Tanner, the left-handed service machine from Lookout Mountain, Tennessee (four sets), and John Newcombe (1) to come up against Stan Smith (4) in the semi-finals.

Big Stan turned on the power and at 8/6, 6/4, 5/4 was serving for the match. Rosewall staved off that crisis, survived a match-point at 5/6 and won the set 9/8. From then on, the tide which had seemed to be engulfing Rosewall turned completely. Smith's forehand weakened under Rosewall's consistent length. Rosewall took the fourth set 6/1 and the fifth 6/3, finishing with a love game.

So Ken got to his fourth Wimbledon Final. He faced an opponent playing in his first Final, Jimmy Connors (3), who, at twenty-one, was little more than half the age of thirty-nine-year-old Ken. Hitherto that year Connors had not looked a likely Finalist. His progress was littered with dropped sets. But once there Connors played devastating tennis. After Rosewall had won his opening service game, Connors blasted his way through ten consecutive games with strokes of unbelievable power and accuracy, hitting the ball early on the return of service and still controlling it down the line. He was at the net in an instant, commanding it with fierce stabbing volleys. After fifty-four minutes the scoreboard read 6/1, 6/1.

The Centre Court crowd was almost silent, as if present at an execution. In the third set Rosewall, ever the trier, slowed the rush, but Connors won it 6/4 to be respectfully, if rather silently acclaimed, as the most crushing winner since Lew Hoad beat Ashley Cooper in 1957. All the emotion was reserved for the hapless Rosewall. Connors said afterwards, 'I just played un-believable tennis today and it couldn't have been at a better time.' But not for Rosewall.

75   A year later the Men's Singles Final scoreboard was again showing 6/1, 6/1 with Connors (1) on court defending his title. But this time there was a differ-ence. That score was against the Champion. His title was turning to Ashe (6), as a rapt and cheering crowd was witnessing the most amazing upset of form and prediction ever seen in a Wimbledon Final.

In the bookmaker's tent, installed in the ground on the tea-lawns for the first time, the scene was that of a miniature stock exchange on a busy day as Ashe, the player who could not win, seemed to be doing just that. On the con-course between the two main courts and the outside ones the electric score-board flashed the scores to scarcely believing eyes.

Connors, who must have felt the almost solid impact of the crowd's con-centration and applause on behalf of Ashe, gained many almost ashamed sup-porters when, having lost nine successive games a voice (possibly with a bet at stake) implored, 'Come on, Connors.' Jimbo replied, 'I'm trying, for Chrissake!'

Ashe had approached the match with a most ingenious tactical plan. He had noted that in the semi-final against Roscoe Tanner, the biggest server in the Championships, Connors had fed on Tanner's pace to unleash an on-slaught of service returns and passing shots. So, in the Final, Ashe deliberately slow-balled Connors, played wide of him, into his body, dinked short, sliced, top-spun, played down the line and across court to weave a web of soft intrigue. Connors's super-powerful game became disorientated.

Throughout this wondrous spell, Ashe was in what he himself calls a 'serene high'. At every change of end he sat by the umpire's chair, deliberately facing away from his opponent, his eyes closed and inducing in himself a form of yoga or self-hypnotism. This shut out all distraction and enabled him to remain on that high plane for much longer than a player can normally achieve.

How's that, Nasty?

It's not nice

Try this for size

Let's get together
next time.

Two wins. ABOVE Jimmy Connors receiving the Doubles trophy on behalf of himself and Nastase, 1973. *Left to right:* Club Chairman, the late Herman David; Connors; Club Secretary Major David Mills; Club President HRH the Duke of Kent.

BELOW *Welcome back.* HRH the Duchess of Kent presents Chrissie Evert with the Challenge Trophy on the occasion of her second Singles win, 1976.

ABOVE Roscoe Tanner, the Chattanooga Choo-Choo, lets off steam...

ABOVE RIGHT...Vilas, his quarter-finals victim at full stretch.

BELOW Virginia Wade sneaks a point on her unhappiest hunting-ground.

It could not last for ever and Connors, determined to end the humiliation, took and held the initiative for nearly a set and a half. He won the third 7/5 and got to 3/0 in the fourth. Knowing heads began to nod, and the odds to slide. Connors was back to form and a Connors in top gear could not be beaten. Wrong again. Ashe re-imposed his skills, winning six of the next seven games to take his first Wimbledon like a conqueror of Everest. He was given the most tumultuous standing ovation seen or heard since the Drobny victory of 1954.

There were other men's singles matches in 1975, 126 of them, many extremely good. But then, and in retrospect, all paled beside the Final.

The quality of the women's line-up was as high as that of the Brough–du Pont era. Chrissie Evert (1), the Champion, found herself against unseeded Betty Stove of the Netherlands in the quarter-final. She made heavy weather of it initially, lost the first set but came back to take the next two, the final one to love. Billie Jean King (3) made certain that Olga Morozova (7) would not provide the upset of the previous year and won 6/3, 6/3. Virginia Wade (6) got to the quarter-finals for the sixth time, where she met Evonne Goolagong (now Mrs Cawley) (4). Virginia gave the usual heart-stopping and often spectacular performance her fans had come to expect. She took an exciting first set 7/5 but lost the equally thrilling second and third sets 3/6, 7/9. The No. 2 seed was a newcomer to the higher ranks, Martina Navratilova, a husky left-hander from Czechoslovakia. She soldiered surely on to the quarter-finals where she found the experience of Margaret Court (5) too much.

What a semi-final line-up! The All-American Chris Evert v. Billie Jean King and the All-Australian Margaret Court v. Evonne Cawley. Billie Jean showed again what a tremendous competitor she is when she came back from a set down, 2/6, with a run of four games to level at one set all. Break-points were liberally sprinkled throughout the third set. First advantage was to Chrissie, who led 3/0 and at 15/40 on her own service Billie Jean's cause looked lost. She again raised her game, saved those two break-points, and a third, gave away no more chances and won six successive games for the match.

Evonne Cawley beat Margaret Court 6/4, 6/4. The score does not fairly reflect an exhilarating match. Evonne was golden. Her strokes flowed to give full rein to her natural genius. And for once her concentration never wavered. Margaret was physically herself but had to use every vestige of her power and athletic ability to try to stem Evonne's flow and to carry the attack to her opponent. Margaret managed a 4/2 lead, but then Evonne struck a winning sequence of four games to take the first set, after Margaret had saved four set-points. The second set was a tug-of-war, evenly balanced until Evonne came from behind with a run of three games for the set and the match.

After two such fine semi-finals, the Final was an anti-climax as far as thrills were concerned. But the tennis played by Billie Jean was masterful. She routed a bewildered Evonne Cawley with a display of serve and volley power of

Sue Barker performs a 'Little Mo'.

The 1975 Final. Arthur Ashe in 'serene high' creates the upset of a century against 'certainty' Jimmy Connors.

which many a man would have been proud, her winning score 6/0, 6/1. The Billie Jean Wimbledon chart now read six Singles titles, putting her equal third with Suzanne Lenglen in the all-time list and behind Mrs Lambert Chambers (7) and Helen Wills Moody (8). Her overall tally of Singles and Doubles titles was now nineteen, level with the record of Elizabeth Ryan, who won all hers in Doubles.

1976   The year 1976 gave Britain a heatwave and lightning fast courts at Wimbledon. Champion Billie Jean King, having announced her retirement from top-flight singles (she came for the Doubles), British hopes were high that the good form shown on the American circuit by Virginia Wade (3), and by new hope, Sue Barker (7), could lead to a British Singles victory.

Virginia had promised much in the past. Her tempestuous talent had blown away senior seeds, but all too often that wind veered against her as she lost the tiller of her own temperament. On her day she has the most forceful game in women's tennis, a game spearheaded by her service. She has to attack. She has a good trained mind, but on court instinct prevails, the instinct to attack. When attack fails and her big shots are not going in, she finds it hard to adapt to circumstances and play a waiting game until the rhythm returns. But in recent years she has been an inspiring captain of the British Wightman Cup team.

The fast courts of Wimbledon 1976 ideally suited Virginia's powerful game. She swept confidently through to the semi-finals, looking vulnerable only in the fourth round when she dropped a set to the challenge of the strong new-comer, Marise Kruger of South Africa. Alas again for British hopes. In the semi-finals she found Evonne Cawley playing her best brand of beautiful tennis and like Evonne against Billie Jean in the previous year's Final, Virginia was made to look a much lesser player. She was beaten 6/1, 6/2.

Sue Barker justified her seeding, reaching the quarter-finals, beating on the way old champion Maria Bueno, back for the first time since 1968. In the quarters Sue met Martina Navratilova (4), with whom she had had several battles on the American circuit. It was a fight, and one which ebbed and flowed. Like Virginia Wade, Sue Barker loves to play an attacking game and she always carried the attack to Martina. But, leading 5/3 in the final set and with Martina seemingly at her last gasp, instead of playing percentage shots Sue went for winners and hit too many losers. Martina was let off the hook and came back to win the set 7/5 and with it the match. At twenty, Sue showed that she was gaining experience and profiting fast. When her forehand is going well she hits prodigious winners. She has shown one hallmark of a champion – a burning desire to excel.

Martina went on to give Chrissie Evert (1) a good semi-final match which the American won 6/4 in the final set. So the Final was between those two young rivals, Chrissie Evert and Evonne Cawley, and it was to produce an occasion to match the Court–King epic of 1970. The issue was in doubt throughout the

We shall fight them on . . . No. 1 Court.
European Zone B Final v. Italy, 1976. The
Lloyd brothers, David (*above*), and John
(*right*) bring off a sensational doubles win to
keep Britain in the fight.

two hours that the girls duelled on the sunny Centre Court. The conditions seemed ideally suited for Evonne with her faster shots, particularly on the backhand, and with her more forceful volleys.

But it was Chrissie who seized the first advantage and kept it to take the first set 6/3. The rallies had been fierce, the shots scintillating. Back came Evonne to break Chrissie's service twice and win the second set 6/4. As in so many matches between Evonne and Chrissie, return of service was often better than service itself. In the long final set the advantage moved briefly one way, then quickly the other until 6/6 was reached. Two points then decided the issue. With Evonne serving, Chrissie got to advantage, and took it. On her own service she reached 40–30 and took that point, and the match. After two hours, her resolution just had the edge which enabled her to allow no mistake at the vital opportunity. Against most expectations Chris Evert was Champion again.

More interest than usual was focused on both the Women's and the Mixed Doubles, which provided Billie Jean with the chance to win her twentieth Wimbledon title to set up an all-time record. She was seeded No. 1 in both, with Sandy Mayer in the Mixed and with Betty Stove in the Women's. Hope soon ended in the Mixed when she and Sandy were beaten in the second round by the combination of Bob Hewitt, that grand old doubles campaigner, and Greer Stevens.

So it was to be all on the Women's. She and Betty Stove got through to their appointed Final place, to be met there by Chris Evert and Martina Navratilova. A 6/1 first set to Chrissie and Martina sent Billie Jean's hopes plunging, but she and Betty recovered to take the second 6/3. The decider was a fight to the last point, which Chrissie and Martina won. So Billie Jean was denied her record at a moment when she probably had greater crowd support than she had had throughout all her years of triumph.

When in 1974 Jimmy Connors ushered in a new era, he looked as if he might be invulnerable for years. Arthur Ashe momentarily stemmed the surge of youth, but in 1976 with many old heroes – Laver, Gonzales and Rosewall – finally bowing out, it became irresistible. Bjorn Borg (4) had already made an impact in 1973 as a seventeen-year-old. 1974 had marked the sudden rise of Guillermo Vilas (6) of Argentina, whose entry into the quarter-finals the following year went almost unnoticed against the epic Ashe–Connors Final.

Borg and Vilas had already had many tough battles around the world and they came together in the 1976 quarter-finals. Here Borg, who had raised his game a class and had not dropped a set in the tournament, kept up his good form with a 6/3, 6/0, 6/2 victory. Jimmy Connors had also been impressive in reaching the quarter-finals without dropping a set, beating on the way Stan Smith (16), the 1972 Champion. In the quarters Connors met up with Roscoe Tanner (7), a player of prodigious power, and at the outset it was felt that if Connors could get past him, he could recapture the title.

Taylor serves at match- and tie-point to
Italy but Panatta's flying forehand volley
drops dead.

Bjorn to be King

It can't be . . . ?

Or can it . . . ?

It is!!!
Borg wins against
Nastase in the 1976
Final.

The first Centenary
Commemorative medal,
designed by Alex Styles
and struck by Garrard,
Crown Jewellers. One
each for Bjorn Borg and
the fifty-one other
living Singles
Champions.

It was a clash of left-handers, with Connors double-fisted on the backhand. The fiery summer and the lightning-fast courts, especially the Centre Court, on which this match was played, favoured Tanner. His game depended so much on his service which, when firing well, was almost the ultimate tennis weapon. Tanner began in blistering form. He squandered his first service game by putting out a volley while Connors was lying on the ground. But from 0/2 he won seven out of eight games. His first service was so fast that it seemed to arc like a tracer bullet from a gun. This fire power is illustrated by his putting fifty per cent of those first serves into court (forty-five out of ninety-two). Nineteen of these were outright aces, and the rest were almost untakable. He did not live by service alone, but it was the serve which crumbled Connors's confidence.

Tanner, who had beaten Connors in the Beckenham semi-final three weeks before, obviously sensed that this was his day, and one could feel his desire to eradicate the memory of the humbling he had received from Connors in the quarter-finals the previous year. He lashed the ball with all his power. His forehand fired continual winners, his volleys were sure and his smashes un-answerable. He took the second set even more easily and led 5/2 in the third. Serving at 0–40, Connors was in the situation of the victim in old Western films, tied to the rails and about to be run over by the train.

But hopeless though the position seemed to everyone else, Jimbo did not submit. The Champion spark, so near extinction, flickered still. He saved four match-points. On the next game he took Tanner's service, for the first time since the opening game of the match. He held his own service to level 5/5. Tanner, serving first, then led 7/6 and suddenly Connors was down again 15/40. This time Tanner hammered home his advantage and the favourite was beaten.

This took him to the semi-final where Borg was to face his fire power. But neither velocity nor accuracy were the same. With his main weapon blunted, even metaphorically knocked out of his hand by some of Borg's service returns, Tanner seemed anxious to get to the net by chipping his approach shot. There, where he had dominated rallies against Connors, he became merely a signpost for the passing shots at which Borg was so adept. Borg's own service was fast and to a good length. It was so consistent that he did not lose it once in the whole match. Borg's performance was the more remarkable in the knowledge that he had pulled a stomach muscle early in the Championship and had needed pain-killing injections before each round that followed.

There were in fact only two service breaks in the entire match, in the first and third sets. The second set was decided on a tie-breaker when the score reached 8/8. So Borg became the first Swede to reach a Wimbledon Final.

His opponent was to be Ilie Nastase (3). The reigning Champion, Arthur Ashe (1), had been put out in the fourth round on Court 3 by up-and-coming Vitas Gerulaitis. In the semi-final Nastase had met Raul Ramirez (8). Nastase for once had been doing his best to concentrate rather than communicate in a serious bid to win the elusive Wimbledon title. But in the semi-final he had returned to his volatile gesturing, especially in his running war with Press photographers. But his tennis genius still flourished in a match which provided some of the best tennis of the tournament, and brought him a win in straight sets. So the Final promised a tennis feast.

For most of the crowd, it was not an occasion for hiding emotion. The blond good looks of Viking demi-god Borg carried even more teenage hearts than those of the dark, handsome Balkan, Nastase, stormy petrel of modern tennis. How much Nastase was affected by the memory of missing a title so near his grasp in 1972, or how much it was the sheer brilliance of Borg on the day, is hard to weigh in the scale. For brilliant Borg was. Nastase began by digging deep into the rich vein of his talent and was soon leading 3/0. In the fourth game, with Borg serving, Nastase had three break-points in five deuces. Had he won this game to lead 4/0 with his own service to follow, the door to the title could well have opened to him.

But Borg, who had again had pain-killing injections before the match, wanted to speed things on his own account. He became a man inspired. He saved that game and, twice in quick succession, had runs of three games to take the set 6/4. He was playing breathtaking tennis, going all out for pace on the fastest surface even the Centre Court had known for years. This sudden switch of ascendancy appeared to drain the spirit of Nastase, who seemed to sense that the prize was again slipping from him. Into the second set with the points brief and the scoreboard flickering fast, 3/2, 4/2, 5/2, 6/2. Two sets to love to Borg.

The third set continued at the same reckless pace, Borg capturing Nastase's service in the opening game and holding his own to lead 2/0. At last Nastase held service and, with service prevailing for a spell, it began to look like a match again. But Borg had that service-break in his pocket and at 4/5 Nastase faced the ultimate truth. He had to break. To his credit he did, after saving a match-point. The score went to 7/7. Borg broke Nastase's service again and held his own, this time to love.

He had become the first Swede to win a Wimbledon Singles crown. It sat well on him. Not only had he won, but he had done so in the grand manner, not losing a set, to become the third youngest holder of the Men's title. The Borg comet, first seen in fiery form in 1973, had now blazed through the Championship and would still be there to light up the Centre Court in Wimbledon's second century.

APPENDICES

$*$ = Holder did not defend.
A = Ambidextrous. Beverly Fleitz was the only finalist to be completely so.
C = Centenary Commemorative medal presented to all living Singles Champions.
F = Win at first attempt.
G = Grand slam, i.e. winner of Australian, French, Wimbledon and USA titles in the same year.
H = Player is left-handed. Double-handed is not included – except for Connors.
LF = Longest final.
M = Only married couple to win Mixed Doubles.
N = Nation wins for first time.
O^1 = Oldest Singles winner; O^2 = 2nd oldest winner, etc.
OR = Oldest Singles runner-up; OR^2 = 2nd oldest Singles runner-up, etc.
SF = Shortest final.
T = Winner of Triple Crown, i.e. Singles, Doubles and Mixed Doubles in the same year.
U = Unseeded. No unseeded player has won a Singles title since full seeding began in 1927.
W = Won Singles, having played through, without losing a set.
Y^1 = Youngest winner; Y^2 = 2nd youngest winner, etc.
YR = Youngest runner-up; YR^2 = 2nd youngest runner-up, etc.

NB(i)   All ages are given in years and days.
NB(ii) Challenge Round introduced in 1878 for men and 1886 for women, and abolished in 1922. Full
        seeding introduced in 1927. Open Championships began in 1968.
NB(iii) Figures in brackets are the seeding numbers.

MEN'S SINGLES – FINALS

	Champion	Runner-up	Score
1877	F S.W. Gore	W. C. Marshall	6/1, 6/2, 6/4
1878	WF P.F. Hadow	S.W. Gore	7/5, 6/1, 9/7
*1879	F J.T. Hartley	V. 'St Leger' Gould	6/2, 6/4, 6/2
1880	O^7 J.T. Hartley *31.187*	H.F. Lawford	6/3, 6/2, 2/6, 6/3
1881	Y^1 W. Renshaw *20.191*	J.T. Hartley	$=SF$ 6/0, 6/1, 6/1
1882	W. Renshaw	E. Renshaw	6/1, 2/6, 4/6, 6/2, 6/2
1883	W. Renshaw	E. Renshaw	2/6, 6/3, 6/3, 4/6, 6/3
1884	W. Renshaw	H.F. Lawford	6/0, 6/4, 9/7
1885	W. Renshaw	H.F. Lawford	7/5, 6/2, 4/6, 7/5
1886	W. Renshaw	H.F. Lawford	6/0, 5/7, 6/3, 6/4
*1887	O^1 H.F. Lawford *45.64*	E. Renshaw	1/6, 6/3, 3/6, 6/4, 6/4
1888	E. Renshaw	H.F. Lawford	6/3, 7/5, 6/0
1889	W. Renshaw	E. Renshaw	6/4, 6/1, 3/6, 6/0
1890	W.J. Hamilton	W. Renshaw	6/8, 6/2, 3/6, 6/1, 6/1
*1891	Y^1 W. Baddeley *19.174*	J. Pim	6/4, 1/6, 7/5, 6/0
1892	W. Baddeley	J. Pim	4/6, 6/3, 6/3, 6/2
1893	J. Pim	W. Baddeley	3/6, 6/1, 6/3, 6/2

	Champion	Runner-up	Score
1894	J. Pim	W. Baddeley	10/8, 6/2, 8/6
*1895	W. Baddeley	W.V. Eaves	4/6, 2/6, 8/6, 6/2, 6/3
1896	H.S. Mahony	W. Baddeley	6/2, 6/8, 5/7, 8/6, 6/3
1897	R.F. Doherty	H.S. Mahony	6/4, 6/4, 6/3
1898	R.F. Doherty	H.L. Doherty	6/3, 6/3, 2/6, 5/7, 6/1
1899	R.F. Doherty	A.W. Gore	1/6, 4/6, 6/2, 6/3, 6/3
1900	R.F. Doherty	S.H. Smith	6/8, 6/3, 6/1, 6/2
1901	A.W. Gore	R.F. Doherty	4/6, 7/5, 6/4, 6/4
1902	H.L. Doherty	A.W. Gore	6/4, 6/3, 3/6, 6/0
1903	H.L. Doherty	F.L. Riseley	7/5, 6/3, 6/0
1904	H.L. Doherty	F.L. Riseley	6/1, 7/5, 8/6
1905	H.L. Doherty	H N.E. Brookes	8/6, 6/2, 6/4
1906	H.L. Doherty	F.L. Riseley	6/4, 4/6, 6/2, 6/3
*1907	N H N.E. Brookes (A'lia)	A.W. Gore	6/4, 6/2, 6/2
*1908	A.W. Gore	H. Roper Barrett	6/3, 6/2, 4/6, 3/6, 6/4
1909	O[1] A.W. Gore 41.182	M.J.G. Ritchie	6/8, 1/6, 6/2, 6/2, 6/2
1910	N A.F. Wilding (NZ)	A.W. Gore	6/4, 7/5, 4/6, 6/2
1911	A.F. Wilding	H. Roper Barrett	6/4, 4/6, 2/6, 6/3 retired
1912	A.F Wilding	O R A.W. Gore 44.188	6/4, 6/4, 4/6, 6/4
1913	A.F. Wilding	M.E. McLoughlin	8/6, 6/3, 10/8
1914	H O[3] N.E. Brookes 36.231	A.F. Wilding	6/4, 6/4, 7/5
1915–18	No competition		
1919	F G.L. Patterson	H N.E. Brookes	6/3, 7/5, 6/2
1920	N F W.T. Tilden (USA)	G.L. Patterson	2/6, 6/3, 6/2, 6/4
1921	W.T. Tilden (USA)	B.I.C. Norton	4/6, 2/6, 6/1, 6/0, 7/5
*1922	G.L. Patterson	R. Lycett	6/3, 6/4, 6/2
1923	W.M. Johnston	F.T. Hunter	6/0, 6/3, 6/1
C 1924	N J. Borotra (Fr)	Y R R. Lacoste 19.363	6/1, 3/6, 6/1, 3/6, 6/4
C 1925	Y[6] R. Lacoste 21.2	J. Borotra	6/3, 6/3, 4/6, 8/6
1926	J. Borotra	H.O. Kinsey	8/6, 6/1, 6/3
C 1927	H. Cochet (4)	J. Borotra (3)	4/6, 4/6, 6/3, 6/4, 7/5
1928	R. Lacoste (2)	H. Cochet (1)	6/1, 4/6, 6/4, 6/2
1929	H. Cochet (1)	J. Borotra (2)	6/4, 6/3, 6/4
1930	O[2] W.T. Tilden (2) 37.145	U W.L. Allison	6/3, 9/7, 6/4
C *1931	Y[2] S.B. Wood (7) w.o. 19.243	F.X. Shields (3)	scratched
C 1932	Y[5] F H.E. Vines (2) 20.278	H.W. Austin (6)	6/4, 6/2, 6/0
C 1933	J.H. Crawford (2)	H.E. Vines (1)	4/6, 11/9, 6/2, 2/6, 6/4
C 1934	F.J. Perry (2)	J.H. Crawford (1)	6/3, 6/0, 7/5
1935	F.J. Perry (1)	G. von Cramm (2)	6/2, 6/4, 6/4
1936	F.J. Perry (1)	G. von Cramm (2)	~SF 6/1, 6/1, 6/0 (20 games)
C *1937	T J.D. Budge (1)	G. von Cramm (2)	6/3, 6/4, 6/2
1938	G T W J.D. Budge (1)	H.W. Austin (2)	6/1, 6/0, 6/3
C *1939	Y[7] T F R.L. Riggs (2) 21.132	E.T. Cooke (6)	2/6, 8/6, 3/6, 6/3, 6/2

	Champion	Runner--up	Score
1940–45	No competition		
C* 1946	O⁹ Y. Petra (5) *30.119*	A G.E. Brown (3)	6/2, 6/4, 7/9, 5/7, 6/4
C 1947	J.A. Kramer (1)	T. Brown (3)	6/1, 6/3, 6/2
C* 1948	R. Falkenburg (7)	A J.E. Bromwich (2)	7/5, 0/6, 6/2, 3/6, 7/5
C 1949	F F.R. Schroeder (1)	H J. Drobny (6)	3/6, 6/0, 6/3, 4/6, 6/4
C* 1950	J.E. Patty (5)	F.A. Sedgman (1)	6/1, 8/10, 6/2, 6/3
C 1951	F R. Savitt (6)	K. McGregor (7)	6/4, 6/4, 6/4
C 1952	T F.A. Sedgman (1)	J. Drobny (2)	4/6, 6/2, 6/3, 6/2
C* 1953	E.V. Seixas (2)	U K. Nielsen	9/7, 6/3, 6/4
C 1954	N H O⁵ J. Drobny (11) (*Eg*) *32.263*	K.R. Rosewall (3)	LF 13/11, 4/6, 6/2, 9/7 (*58 games*)
C 1955	W M.A. Trabert (1)	U K. Nielsen	6/3, 7/5, 6/1
C* 1956	Y⁸ L.A. Hoad (1) *21.225*	K.R. Rosewall (2)	6/2, 4/6, 7/5, 6/4
1957	L.A. Hoad (1)	Y R³ A.J. Cooper (2) *20.293*	6/2, 6/1, 6/2
C* 1958	Y⁹ A.J. Cooper (1) *21.291*	H N.A. Fraser (4)	3/6, 6/3, 6/4, 13/11
C* 1959	A. Olmedo (1)	U H R.G. Laver	6/4, 6/3, 6/4
C* 1960	H N.A. Fraser (1)	H R.G. Laver (3)	6/4, 3/6, 9/7, 7/5
C 1961	H R.G. Laver (2)	Y R² C.R. McKinley (8) *20.187*	6/3, 6/1, 6/4
1962	G H R.G. Laver (1)	U M.F. Mulligan	6/2, 6/2, 6/1
C* 1963	W C.R. McKinley (4)	U F.S. Stolle	9/7, 6/1, 6/4
C 1964	R.S. Emerson (1)	F.S. Stolle (6)	6/4, 12/10, 4/6, 6/3
1965	R.S. Emerson (1)	F.S. Stolle (2)	6/2, 6/4, 6/4
C 1966	N M. Santana (4) (*Sp*)	R.D. Ralston (6)	6/4, 11/9, 6/4
C 1967	J.D. Newcombe (1)	U W.P. Bungert	6/3, 6/1, 6/1
1968	H R.G. Laver (1)	H A.D. Roche (15)	6/3, 6/4, 6/2
1969	G O⁸ H R.G. Laver (1) *30.330*	J.D. Newcombe (6)	6/4, 5/7, 6/4, 6/4
1970	J.D. Newcombe (2)	K.R. Rosewall (5)	5/7, 6/3, 6/2, 3/6, 6/1
1971	J.D. Newcombe (2)	S.R. Smith (4)	6/3, 5/7, 2/6, 6/4, 6/4
C* 1972	S.R. Smith (1)	I. Nastase (2)	4/6, 6/3, 6/3, 4/6, 7/5
C* 1973	N J. Kodes (2) (*Cz*)	A. Metreveli (4)	6/1, 9/8, 6/3
C 1974	H Y¹⁰ J.S. Connors (3) *21.307*	O R² K.R. Rosewall (9) *39.246*	6/1, 6/1, 6/4
C 1975	O⁶ A.R. Ashe (6) *31.360*	H J.S. Connors (1)	6/1, 6/1, 5/7, 6/4
C 1976	Y³ W N B. Borg (4) (*Swe*) *20.27*	I. Nastase (3)	6/4, 6/2, 9/7

NB: Challenge Round introduced in 1870, and abolished in 1922. Full seeding introduced in 1927. Open Championships began in 1968.

MEN'S DOUBLES–FINALS

	Champions	Runners-up	Score
1879	L.R. Erskine/ H.F. Lawford	F. Durant/ G.E. Tabor	4/6, 6/4, 6/5, 6/2, 3/6, 3/6, 5/6, 1
1880	W. Renshaw/ E. Renshaw	O.E. Woodhouse/ C.J. Cole	6/1, 6/4, 6/0, 6/8, 6/3
1881	W. Renshaw E. Renshaw	W.J. Down/ H. Vaughan	Played at Oxford 6/0, 6/0, 6/4
1882	J.T. Hartley/ R.T. Richardson	J.G. Horn/ C.B. Russell	6/2, 6/1, 6/0
1883	C.W. Grinstead/ C.E. Welldon	C.B. Russell/ R.T. Milford	3/6, 6/1, 6/3, 6/4

	Champions	Runners-up	Score
1884	W. Renshaw/ E. Renshaw	E.W. Lewis/ E.L. Williams	6/3, 3/6, 6/1, 1/6, 6/4
1885	W. Renshaw/ E. Renshaw	C.E. Farrar/ A.J. Stanley	6/3, 6/3, 10/8
1886	W. Renshaw/ E. Renshaw	C.E. Farrar/ A.J. Stanley	6/3, 6/3, 4/6, 7/5
1887	H.W.W. Wilberforce/ The Hon P.B. Lyon	J.H. Crispe/ E. Barratt Smith	7/5, 6/3, 6/2
1888	W. Renshaw/ E. Renshaw	H.W.W. Wilberforce/ The Hon P.B. Lyon	2/6, 1/6, 6/3, 6/4, 6/3
1889	W. Renshaw/ E. Renshaw	E.W. Lewis/ G.W. Hillyard	6/4, 6/4, 3/6, 0/6, 6/1
1890	J. Pim/ F.O. Stoker	E.W. Lewis/ G.W. Hillyard	6/0, 7/5, 6/4
1891	W. Baddeley/ H. Baddeley	J. Pim/ F.O. Stoker	6/1, 6/3, 1/6, 6/2
1892	E.W. Lewis/ H.S. Barlow	W. Baddeley/ H. Baddeley	4/6, 6/2, 8/6, 6/4
1893	J. Pim/ F.O. Stoker	E.W. Lewis/ H.S. Barlow	4/6, 6/3, 6/1, 2/6, 6/0
1894	W. Baddeley/ H. Baddeley	H.S. Barlow/ C.H. Martin	5/7, 7/5, 4/6, 6/3, 8/6
1895	W. Baddeley/ H. Baddeley	E.W. Lewis/ W.V. Eaves	8/6, 5/7, 6/4, 6/3
1896	W. Baddeley/ H. Baddeley	R.F. Doherty/ H.A. Nisbet	1/6, 3/6, 6/4, 6/2, 6/1
1897	R.F. Doherty/ H.L. Doherty	W. Baddeley/ H. Baddeley	6/4, 4/6, 8/6, 6/4
1898	R.F. Doherty/ H.L. Doherty	H.A. Nisbet/ C. Hobart	6/4, 6/4, 6/2
1899	R.F. Doherty/ H.L. Doherty	H.A. Nisbet/ C. Hobart	7/5, 6/0, 6/2
1900	R.F. Doherty/ H.L. Doherty	H. Roper Barrett/ H.A. Nisbet	9/7, 7/5, 4/6, 3/6, 6/3
1901	R.F. Doherty/ H.L. Doherty	D.F. Davis/ H. Ward	4/6, 6/2, 6/3, 9/7
1902	S.H. Smith/ F.L. Riseley	R.F. Doherty/ H.L. Doherty	4/6, 8/6, 6/3, 4/6, 11/9
1903	R.F. Doherty/ H.L. Doherty	S.H. Smith/ F.L. Riseley	6/4, 6/4, 6/4
1904	R.F. Doherty/ H.L. Doherty	S.H. Smith/ F.L. Riseley	6/1, 6/2, 6/4
1905	R.F. Doherty/ H.L. Doherty	S.H. Smith/ F.L. Riseley	6/2, 6/4, 6/8, 6/3
1906	S.H. Smith/ F.L. Riseley	R.F. Doherty/ H.L. Doherty	6/8, 6/4, 5/7, 6/3, 6/3
1907	N.E. Brookes/ A.F. Wilding	B.C. Wright/ K. Behr	6/4, 6/4, 6/2
1908	A.F. Wilding/ M.J.G. Ritchie	A.W Gore/ H. Roper Barrett	6/1, 6/2, 1/6, 1/6, 9/7
1909	A.W. Gore/ H. Roper Barrett	S.N. Doust/ H.A. Parker	6/2, 6/1, 6/4
1910	A.F. Wilding/ M.J.G. Ritchie	A.W. Gore/ H. Roper Barrett	6/1, 6/1, 6/2
1911	A.H. Gobert/ M. Decugis	M.J.G. Ritchie/ A.F Wilding	9/7, 5/7, 6/3, 2/6, 6/2
1912	H. Roper Barrett/ C.P. Dixon	A.H. Gobert/ M. Decugis	3/6, 6/3, 6/4, 7/5
1913	H. Roper Barrett/ C.P. Dixon	F.W. Rahe/ H. Kleinschroth	6/2, 6/4, 4/6, 6/2

	Champions	Runners-up	Score
1914	N.E. Brookes/ A.F. Wilding	H. Roper Barrett/ C.P. Dixon	6/1, 6/1, 5/7, 8/6
1915–18	No competition		
1919	R.V. Thomas/ P. O'Hara Wood	R. Lycett/ R.W. Heath	6/4, 6/2, 4/6, 6/2
1920	R.N. Williams/ C.S. Garland	A.R.F. Kingscote/ J.C. Parke	4/6, 6/4, 7/5, 6/2
1921	R. Lycett/ M. Woosnam	F.G. Lowe/ A.H. Lowe	6/3, 6/0, 7/5
1922	J.O. Anderson/ R. Lycett	G.L. Patterson/ P. O'Hara Wood	3/6, 7/9, 6/4, 6/3, 11/9
1923	R. Lycett/ A. Godfree	Count de Gomar/ E. Flaquer	6/3, 6/4, 3/6, 6/3
1924	V. Richards/ F.T. Hunter	R.N. Williams/ W.M. Washburn	6/3, 3/6, 8/10, 8/6, 6/3
1925	R. Lacoste/ J. Borotra	H. Hennessey/ R. Casey	6/4, 11/9, 4/6, 1/6, 6/3
1926	H. Cochet/ J. Brugnon	V. Richards/ H.O. Kinsey	7/5, 4/6, 6/3, 6/2
1927	F.T. Hunter/ W.T. Tilden	J. Brugnon/ H. Cochet	1/6, 4/6, 8/6, 6/3, 6/4
1928	H. Cochet/ J. Brugnon	G.L. Patterson/ J.B. Hawkes	13/11, 6/4, 6/4
1929	U W.L. Allison/ J. Van Ryn	J.C. Gregory/ I.G. Collins	6/4, 5/7, 6/3, 10/12, 6/4
1930	W.L. Allison/ J. Van Ryn	J.H. Doeg/ G.M. Lott	6/3, 6/3, 6/2
1931	G.M. Lott/ J. Van Ryn	H. Cochet/ J. Brugnon	6/2, 10/8, 9/11, 3/6, 6/3
1932	J. Borotra/ J. Brugnon	G.P. Hughes/ F.J. Perry	6/0, 4/6, 3/6, 7/5, 7/5
1933	J. Borotra/ J. Brugnon	U R. Nunoi/ J. Sato	4/6, 6/3, 6/3, 7/5
1934	G.M. Lott/ L.R. Stoefen	J. Borotra/ J. Brugnon	6/2, 6/3, 6/4
1935	J.H. Crawford/ A.K. Quist	W.L Allson/ J. Van Ryn	6/3, 5/7, 6/2, 5/7, 7/5
1936	G.P. Hughes/ C.R.D. Tuckey	U C.E. Hare/ F.H.D. Wilde	6/4, 3/6, 7/9, 6/1, 6/4
1937	J.D. Budge/ C.G. Mako	G.P. Hughes/ C.R.D. Tuckey	6/0, 6/4, 6/8, 6/1
1938	J.D. Budge/ C.G. Mako	H. Henkel/ G. von Metaxa	6/4, 3/6, 6/3, 8/6
1939	E.T. Cooke/ R.L. Riggs	C.E. Hare/ F.H.D. Wilde	6/3, 3/6, 6/3, 9/7
1940–45	No competition		
1946	T. Brown/ J.A. Kramer	G.E. Brown/ D. Pails	6/4, 6/4, 6/2
1947	R. Falkenburg/ J.A. Kramer	U A.J. Mottram/ O.W. Sidwell	8/6, 6/3, 6/3
1948	J.E. Bromwich/ F.A. Sedgman	T. Brown/ G. Mulloy	5/7, 7/5, 7/5, 9/7
1949	R.P. Gonzales/ F.A. Parker	G. Mulloy/ F.R. Schroeder	6/4, 6/4, 6/2
1950	J.E. Bromwich/ A.K. Quist	G.E. Brown/ O.W. Sidwell	7/5, 3/6, 6/3, 3/6, 6/2
1951	K. McGregor/ F.A. Sedgman	J. Drobny/ E.W. Sturgess	3/6, 6/2, 6/3, 3/6, 6/3
1952	G K. McGregor/ G F.A. Sedgman	E.V. Seixas/ E.W. Sturgess	6/3, 7/5, 6/4

	Champions	Runners-up	Score
1953	L.A. Hoad/ K.R. Rosewall	R.N. Hartwig/ M.G. Rose	6/4, 7/5, 4/6, 7/5
1954	R.N. Hartwig/ M.G. Rose	E.V. Seixas/ M.A. Trabert	6/4, 6/4, 3/6, 6/4
1955	R.N. Hartwig/ L.A. Hoad	N.A. Fraser/ K.R. Rosewall	7/5, 6/4, 6/3
1956	L.A. Hoad/ K.R. Rosewall	U N. Pietrangeli/ O. Sirola	7/5, 6/2, 6/1
1957	U G. Mulloy/ J.E. Patty	N.A. Fraser/ L.A. Hoad	8/10, 6/4, 6/4, 6/4
1958	U S. Davidson/ U. Schmidt	A.J. Cooper/ N.A. Fraser	6/4, 6/4, 8/6
1959	R.S. Emerson/ N.A. Fraser	R.G. Laver/ R. Mark	8/6, 6/3, 14/16, 9/7
1960	U R.H. Osuna/ R.D. Ralston	U M.G. Davies/ R.K. Wilson	7/5, 6/3, 10/8
1961	R.S. Emerson/ N.A. Fraser	U R.A.J. Hewitt/ F.S. Stolle	6/4, 6/8, 6/4, 6/8, 8/6
1962	R.A.J. Hewitt/ F.S. Stolle	U B. Jovanovic/ N. Pilic	6/2, 5/7, 6/2, 6/4
1963	U R.H. Osuna/ A. Palafox	U J.C. Barclay/ P. Darmon	4/6, 6/2, 6/2, 6/2
1964	R.A.J. Hewitt/ F.S. Stolle	R.S. Emerson/ K.N. Fletcher	7/5, 11/9, 6/4
1965	J.D. Newcombe/ A.D. Roche	K.N. Fletcher/ R.A.J. Hewitt	7/5, 6/3, 6/4
1966	U K.N. Fletcher/ J.D. Newcombe	W.W. Bowrey/ O.K. Davidson	6/3, 6/4, 3/6, 6/3
1967	R.A.J. Hewitt/ F.D. McMillan	R.S. Emerson/ K.N. Fletcher	6/2, 6/3, 6/4
1968	J.D. Newcombe/ A.D. Roche	K.R. Rosewall/ F.S. Stolle	3/6, 8/6, 5/7, 14/12, 6/3
1969	J.D. Newcombe/ A.D. Roche	T.S. Okker/ M.C. Riessen	7/5, 11/9, 6/3
1970	J.D. Newcombe/ A.D. Roche	K.R. Rosewall/ F.S. Stolle	10/8, 6/3, 6/1
1971	U R.S. Emerson/ R.G. Laver	U A.R. Ashe/ R.D. Ralston	4/6, 9/7, 6/8, 6/4, 6/4
1972	R.A.J Hewitt/ F.D. McMillan	S.R. Smith/ E.J. Van Dillen	6/2, 6/2, 9/7
1973	J.S. Connors/ I. Nastase	J.R. Cooper/ N.A. Fraser	3/6, 6/3, 6/4, 8/9, 6/1
1974	J.D. Newcombe/ A.D. Roche	R.C. Lutz/ S.R. Smith	8/6, 6/4, 6/4
1975	U V. Gerulatis/ A. Mayer	C. Dowdeswell/ A.J. Stone	7/5, 8/6, 6/4
1976	B.E. Gottfried/ R. Ramirez	U R.L. Case/ G. Masters	3/6, 6/3, 8/6, 2/6, 7/5

NB: Challenge Round introduced in 1886, and abolished in 1922. Open Championships began in 1968.

WOMEN'S SINGLES—FINALS

	Champion	Runner-up	Score
1884	Y⁶ F Miss M. Watson *19.284*	Miss L. Watson	6/8, 6/3, 6/3
1885	W Miss M. Watson	Miss B. Bingley	6/1, 7/5
1886	W Miss B. Bingley	Miss M. Watson	6/3, 6/3
1887	Y¹ W F Miss L. Dod *15.285*	Miss B. Bingley	6/2, 6/0
1888	Miss L. Dod	Mrs G.W. Hillyard	6/3, 6/3
*1889	Mrs G.W. Hillyard	Miss L. Rice	4/6, 8/6, 6/4

	Champion	Runner-up	Score
*1890	W Miss L. Rice	Miss M. Jacks	6/4, 6/1
*1891	W Miss L. Dod	Mrs G.W. Hillyard	6/2, 6/1
1892	Miss L. Dod	Mrs G.W. Hillyard	6/1, 6/1
1893	Miss L. Dod	Mrs G.W. Hillyard	6/8, 6/1, 6/4
*1894	W Mrs G.W. Hillyard	Miss L. Austin	6/1, 6/1
*1895	Miss C. Cooper	Miss H. Jackson	7/5, 8/6
1896	Miss C. Cooper	Mrs W.H. Pickering	6/2, 6/3
1897	Mrs G.W. Hillyard	Miss C. Cooper	5/7, 7/5, 6/2
*1898	Miss C. Cooper	Miss L. Martin	6/4, 6/4
1899	Mrs G.W. Hillyard	Miss C. Cooper	6/2, 6/3
1900	O^2 Mrs G.W. Hillyard 36.242	Miss C. Cooper	4/6, 6/4, 6/4
1901	W Mrs A. Sterry	Mrs G.W. Hillyard	6/2, 6/2
1902	Miss M.E. Robb	Mrs A. Sterry	7/5, 6/1
*1903	Miss D.K. Douglass	Miss E.W. Thomson	4/6, 6/4, 6/2
1904	Miss D.K. Douglass	Mrs A. Sterry	6/0, 6/3
1905	Y^3 N W F Miss M.G. Sutton (USA) 18.286	Miss D.K. Douglass	6/3, 6/4
1906	W Miss D.K. Douglass	Miss M.G. Sutton	6/3, 9/7
1907	W Miss M.G. Sutton	Mrs Lambert Chambers	6/1, 6/4
*1908	O^1 W Mrs A. Sterry 37.296	Miss A.M. Morton	6/4, 6/4
*1909	Miss D.P. Boothby	Miss A.M. Morton	6/4, 4/6, 8/6
1910	W Mrs Lambert Chambers	Miss D.P. Boothby	6/2, 6/2
1911	Mrs Lambert Chambers	Miss D.P. Boothby	SF 6/0, 6/0 (12 games)
*1912	O^4 Mrs D.R. Larcombe 33.27	Mrs A. Sterry	6/3, 6/1
*1913	W Mrs Lambert Chambers	Mrs R.J. McNair	6/0, 6/4
1914	O^3 Mrs Lambert Chambers 35.304	Mrs D.R. Larcombe	7/5, 6/4
1915–18	No competition		
1919	Y^9 N F Miss S. Lenglen (Fr) 20.42	Mrs Lambert Chambers	10/8, 4/6, 9/7
1920	T Miss S. Lenglen	OR Mrs Lambert Chambers 41.302	6/3, 6/0
1921	Miss S. Lenglen	Miss E. Ryan	6/2, 6/0
1922	T W Miss S. Lenglen	Mrs M. Mallory	6/2, 6/0
1923	W Miss S. Lenglen	Miss K. McKane	6/2, 6/2
C 1924	Miss K. McKane	Miss H. Wills	4/6, 6/4, 6/4
1925	T W Miss S. Lenglen	Miss J. Fry	6/2, 6/0
1926	Mrs. L.A. Godfree	Miss L. de Alvarez	6/2, 4/6, 6/3
C 1927	Y^{11} Miss H. Wills (1) 21.269	Miss L. de Alvarez (4)	6/2, 6/4
1928	W Miss H. Wills (1)	Miss L. de Alvarez (2)	6/3, 6/3
1929	W Miss H. Wills (1)	Miss H.H. Jacobs (5)	6/1, 6/2
1930	W Mrs F.S. Moody (1)	OR^2 Miss E. Ryan (8) 38.149	6/2, 6/2
*1931	N Miss C. Aussem (1) (Ger)	Miss H. Krahwinkel (4)	6/2, 7/5
*1932	W Mrs F.S. Moody (1)	Miss H.H. Jacobs (5)	6/3, 6/1
1933	Mrs F.S. Moody (1)	Miss D.E. Round (2)	6/4, 6/8, 6/3
C *1934	Miss D.E. Round (2)	Miss H.H. Jacobs (1)	6/2, 5/7, 6/3
1935	Mrs F.S. Moody (4)	Miss H.H. Jacobs (3)	6/3, 3/6, 7/5
C *1936	Miss H.H. Jacobs (2)	Mrs S. Sperling (5)	6/2, 4/6, 7/5
1937	Miss D.E. Round (7)	Miss J. Jedrzejowska (4)	6/2, 2/6, 7/5
*1938	O^5 W Mrs F.S. Moody (1) 32.269	U Miss H.H. Jacobs	6/4, 6/0
C *1939	T W Miss A. Marble (1)	H Miss K.E. Stammers (6)	6/2, 6/0
1940–45	No competition		
C *1946	W F Miss P.M. Betz (1)	Miss A.L. Brough (3)	6/2, 6/4
C *1947	W Miss M.E. Osborne (1)	Miss D.J. Hart (3)	6/2, 6/4
C 1948	T Miss A.L. Brough (2)	Miss D.J. Hart (4)	6/3, 8/6
1949	Miss A.L. Brough (1)	Mrs W. du Pont (2)	10/8, 1/6, 10/8
1950	T Miss A.L. Brough (1)	Mrs W. du Pont (2)	6/1, 3/6, 6/1
c 1951	T W D.J. Hart (3)	Miss S.J. Fry (4)	6/1 6/0
1952	Y^2 F Miss M. Connolly (2) 17.291	Miss A.L. Brough (4)	7/5, 6/3
1953	G W Miss M. Connolly (1)	Miss D.J. Hart (2)	8/6, 7/5
1954	W Miss M. Connolly (1)	Miss A.L. Brough (4)	6/2, 7/5
*1955	O^6 W Miss A.L. Brough (2) 32.113	A Mrs J.G. Fleitz (3)	7/5, 8/6
c 1956	Miss S.J. Fry (5)	Miss A. Buxton (6)	6/3, 6/1
c *1957	W Miss A. Gibson (1)	Miss D.R. Hard (5)	6/3, 6/2
1958	O^8 Miss A. Gibson (1) 30.314	U Miss A. Mortimer	8/6, 6/2
c *1959	N Y^6 Miss M.E. Bueno (6) (Braz) 19.266	Miss D.R. Hard (4)	6/4, 6/3
1960	Miss M.E. Bueno (1)	Miss S. Reynolds (8)	8/6, 6/0
c *1961	Miss A. Mortimer (7)	Miss C.C. Truman (6)	4/6, 6/4, 7/5
c 1962	Y^5 W Mrs J.R. Susman (8) 19.208	U Mrs V. Sukova	6/4, 6/4
c *1963	N Y^{10} Miss M. Smith (1) (A'lia) 20.357	U Miss B.J. Moffitt	6/3, 6/4
1964	Miss M.E. Bueno (2)	Miss M. Smith (1)	6/4, 7/9, 6/3

WOMEN'S SINGLES—FINALS

		Champion	Runner-up	Score
1965		*W* Miss M. Smith (2)	Miss M.E. Bueno (1)	6/4, 7/5
1966		Mrs L.W. King (4)	Miss M.E. Bueno (2)	6/3, 3/6, 6/1
1967		*T W* Mrs L.W. King (1)	*H* Mrs P.F. Jones (3)	6/3, 6/4
1968		Mrs L.W. King (1)	Miss J.A.M. Tegart (7)	9/7, 7/5
1969		*H O*[9] Mrs P.F. Jones (4) *30.260*	Mrs L.W. King (2)	3/6, 6/3, 6/2
1970		*G* Mrs B.M. Court (1)	Mrs L.W. King (2)	*LF* 14/12, 11/9 (*46 games*)
1971		*Y*[8] Miss E.F. Goolagong (3) *19.337*	Mrs B.M. Court (1)	6/4, 6/1
	1972	Mrs L.W. King (2)	Miss E.F. Goolagong (1)	6/3, 6/3
1973		*T* Mrs L.W. King (2)	Miss C.M. Evert (4)	6/0, 7/5
1974		*Y*[4] Miss C.M. Evert (2) *19.196*	Mrs O. Morozova (8)	6/0, 6/4
1975		*O*[7] Mrs L.W. King (3) *31.224*	Mrs R. Cawley (4)	6/0, 6/1
1976		Miss C.M. Evert (1)	Mrs R. Cawley (2)	6/3, 4/6, 8/6

WOMEN'S DOUBLES—FINALS

	Champions	Runners-up	Score
1913	Mrs R.J. McNair/ Miss D.P. Boothby	Mrs A. Sterry/ Mrs Lambert Chambers	6/4, 2/4 (retd)
1914	Miss E. Ryan/ Miss A.M. Morton	Mrs D.R. Larcombe/ Mrs F.J. Hannam	6/1, 6/3
1915–18	No competition		
1919	Miss S. Lenglen/ Miss E. Ryan	Mrs Lambert Chambers/ Mrs D.R. Larcombe	4/6, 7/5, 6/3
1920	Miss S. Lenglen/ Miss E. Ryan	Mrs Lambert Chambers/ Mrs D.R. Larcombe	6/4, 6/0
1921	Miss S. Lenglen/ Miss E. Ryan	Mrs A.E. Beamish/ Mrs I.E. Peacock	6/1, 6/2
1922	Miss S. Lenglen/ Miss E. Ryan	Mrs A.D. Stocks/ Miss K. McKane	6/0, 6/4
1923	Miss S. Lenglen/ Miss E. Ryan	Miss J. Austin/ Miss E.L. Colyer	6/3, 6/1
1924	Mrs G.W. Wightman/ Miss H. Wills	Mrs B.C. Covell/ Miss K. McKane	6/4, 6/4
1925	Miss S. Lenglen/ Miss E. Ryan	Mrs A.V. Bridge/ Mrs C.G. McIlquham	6/2, 6/2
1926	Miss E. Ryan/ Miss M.K. Browne	Mrs L.A. Godfree/ Miss E.L. Colyer	6/1, 6/1
1927	Miss H. Wills/ Miss E. Ryan	Miss E.L. Heine/ Mrs I.E. Peacock	6/3, 6/2
1928	Mrs Holcroft-Watson/ Miss P. Saunders	Miss E.H. Harvey/ Miss E.B. Bennett	6/2, 6/3
1929	Mrs Holcroft-Watson/ Mrs L.R.C. Michell	Mrs B.C. Covell/ Mrs D.C. Shepherd-Barron	6/4, 8/6
1930	Mrs F.S. Moody/ Miss E. Ryan	Miss E. Cross/ Miss S. Palfrey	6/2, 9/7
1931	*U* Mrs D.C. Shepherd-Barron/ Miss P.E. Mudford	Miss D. Metaxa/ Miss J. Sigart	3/6, 6/3, 6/4
1932	Miss D. Metaxa/ Miss J. Sigart	Miss E. Ryan/ Miss H.H. Jacobs	6/4, 6/3
1933	Mrs R. Mathieu/ Miss E. Ryan	*U* Miss F. James/ Miss A.M. Yorke	6/2, 9/11, 6/4
1934	Mrs R. Mathieu/ Miss E. Ryan	*U* Mrs D. Andrus/ Mrs S. Henrotin	6/3, 6/3
1935	Miss F. James/ Miss K.E. Stammers	Mrs R. Mathieu/ Mrs S. Sperling	6/1, 6/4
1936	Miss F. James/ Miss K.E. Stammers	Mrs S.P. Fabyan/ Miss H.H. Jacobs	6/2, 6/1
1937	Mrs R. Mathieu/ Miss A.M. Yorke	*U* Mrs M.R. King/ Mrs J.B. Pitman	6/3, 6/3

	Champions	Runners-up	Score
1938	Mrs S.P. Fabyan/ Miss A. Marble	Mrs R. Mathieu/ Miss A.M. Yorke	6/2, 6/3
1939	Mrs S.P. Fabyan/ Miss A. Marble	Miss H.H. Jacobs/ Miss A.M. Yorke	6/1, 6/0
1940–45	No competition		
1946	Miss A.L. Brough/ Miss M.E. Osborne	Miss P.M. Betz/ Miss D.J. Hart	6/3, 2/6, 6/3
1947	Miss D.J. Hart/ Mrs P.C. Todd	Miss A.L. Brough/ Miss M.E. Osborne	3/6, 6/4, 7/5
1948	Miss A.L. Brough/ Mrs W. du Pont	Miss D.J. Hart/ Mrs P.C. Todd	6/3, 3/6, 6/3
1949	Miss A.L. Brough/ Mrs W. du Pont	Miss G. Moran/ Mrs P.C. Todd	8/6, 7/5
1950	Miss A.L. Brough/ Mrs W. du Pont	Miss S.J. Fry/ Miss D.J. Hart	6/4, 5/7, 6/1
1951	Miss S.J. Fry/ Miss D.J. Hart	Miss A.L. Brough/ Mrs W. du Pont	6/3, 13/11
1952	Miss S.J. Fry/ Miss D.J. Hart	Miss A.L. Brough/ Miss M. Connolly	8/6, 6/3
1953	Miss S.J. Fry/ Miss D.J. Hart	Miss M. Connolly/ Miss J. Sampson	6/0, 6/0
1954	Miss A.L. Brough/ Mrs W. du Pont	Miss S.J. Fry/ Miss D.J. Hart	4/6, 9/7, 6/3
1955	Miss A. Mortimer/ Miss J.A. Shilcock	Miss S.J. Bloomer/ Miss P.E. Ward	7/5, 6/1
1956	Miss A. Buxton/ Miss A. Gibson	U Miss F. Muller/ Miss D.G. Seeney	6/1, 8/6
1957	Miss A. Gibson/ Miss D.R. Hard	Mrs K. Hawton/ Mrs T.D. Long	6/1, 6/2
1958	Miss M.E. Bueno/ Miss A. Gibson	U Mrs W. du Pont/ Miss M. Varner	6/3, 7/5
1959	Miss J. Arth/ Miss D.R. Hard	Mrs J.G. Fleitz/ Miss C.C. Truman	2/6, 6/2, 6/3
1960	G Miss M.E. Bueno/ Miss D.R. Hard	Miss S. Reynolds/ Miss R. Schuurman	6/4, 6/0
1961	U Miss K. Hantze/ Miss B.J. Moffitt	Miss J. Lehane/ Miss M. Smith	6/3, 6/4
1962	Miss B.J. Moffitt/ Mrs J.R. Susman	Mrs L.E.G. Price/ Miss R. Schuurman	5/7, 6/3, 7/5
1963	Miss M.E. Bueno/ Miss D.R. Hard	Miss R.A. Ebbern/ Miss M. Smith	8/6, 9/7
1964	Miss M. Smith/ Miss L.R. Turner	Miss B.J. Moffitt/ Mrs J.R. Susman	7/5, 6/2
1965	Mrs M.E. Bueno/ Miss B.J. Moffitt	U Miss F. Durr/ Miss J. Lieffrig	6/2, 7/5
1966	Miss M.E. Bueno/ Miss N. Richey	Miss M. Smith/ Miss J.A.M. Tegart	6/3, 4/6, 6/4
1967	Miss R. Casals/ Mrs L.W. King	Miss M.E. Bueno/ Miss N. Richey	9/11, 6/4, 6/2
1968	Miss R. Casals/ Mrs L.W. King	Miss F. Durr/ Mrs P.F. Jones	3/6, 6/4, 7/5
1969	Mrs B.M. Court/ Miss J.A.M. Tegart	U Miss P.S.A. Hogan/ Miss M. Michel	9/7, 6/2
1970	Miss R. Casals/ Mrs L.W. King	Miss F. Durr/ Miss S.V. Wade	6/2, 6/3
1971	Miss R. Casals/ Mrs L.W. King	Mrs B.M. Court/ Miss E.F. Goolagong	6/3, 6/2
1972	Mrs L.W. King/ Miss B.F. Stove	Mrs D.E. Dalton/ Miss F. Durr	6/2, 4/6, 6/3
1973	Miss R. Casals/ Mrs L.W. King	Miss F. Durr/ Miss B.F. Stove	6/1, 4/6, 7/5

WOMEN'S DOUBLES—FINALS

	Champions	Runners-up	Score
1974	*U* Miss E.F. Goolagong/ Miss M. Michel	*U* Mrs H.F. Gourlay/ Miss K. M. Krantzcke	2/6, 6/4, 6/3
1975	*U* Miss A.K. Kiyomura/ Miss K. Sawamatsu	*U* Miss F. Durr/ Miss B.F. Stove	7/5, 1/6, 7/5
1976	Miss C.M. Evert/ Miss M. Navratilova	Mrs L.W. King/ Miss B.F. Stove	6/1, 3/6, 7/5

NB: Open Championships began in 1968.

MIXED DOUBLES—FINALS

	Champions	Runners-up	Score
1913	H. Crisp/ Mrs C.O. Tuckey	J.C. Parke/ Mrs D.R. Larcombe	3/6, 5/3 (retd)
1914	J.C. Parke/ Mrs D.R. Larcombe	A.F. Wilding/ Miss M. Broquedis	4/6, 6/4, 6/2
1915–18	No competition		
1919	R. Lycett/ Miss E. Ryan	A.D. Prebble/ Mrs Lambert Chambers	6/0, 6/0
1920	G.L. Patterson/ Miss S. Lenglen	R. Lycett/ Miss E. Ryan	7/5, 6/3
1921	R. Lycett/ Miss E. Ryan	M. Woosnam/ Miss P.L. Howkins	6/3, 6/1
1922	P. O'Hara Wood/ Miss S. Lenglen	R. Lycett/ Miss E. Ryan	6/4, 6/3
1923	R. Lycett/ Miss E. Ryan	L.S. Deane/ Mrs D.C. Shepherd-Barron	6/4, 7/5
1924	J.B. Gilbert/ Miss K. McKane	L.A. Godfree/ Mrs D.C. Shepherd-Barron	6/3, 3/6, 6/3
1925	J. Borotra/ Miss S. Lenglen	H.L. de Morpurgo/ Miss E. Ryan	6/3, 6/3
1926	*M* L.A. Godfree/ Mrs L.A. Godfree	H.O. Kinsey/ Miss M.K. Browne	6/3, 6/4
1927	F.T. Hunter/ Miss E. Ryan	L.A. Godfree/ Mrs L.A. Godfree	8/6, 6/0
1928	P.D.B. Spence/ Miss E. Ryan	*U* J.H. Crawford/ Miss D. Akhurst	7/5, 6/4
1929	F.T. Hunter/ Miss H. Wills	*U* I.G. Collins/ Miss J. Fry	6/1, 6/4
1930	J.H. Crawford/ Miss E. Ryan	*U* D. Prenn/ Miss H. Krahwinkel	6/1, 6/3
1931	*U* G.M. Lott/ Mrs L.A. Harper	*U* I.G. Collins/ Miss J.C. Ridley	6/3, 1/6, 6/1
1932	E. Maier/ Miss E. Ryan	H.C. Hopman/ Miss J. Sigart	7/5, 6/2
1933	*U* G. von Cramm/ Miss H. Krahwinkel	N.G. Farquharson/ Miss M. Heeley	7/5, 8/6
1934	*U* R. Miki/ Miss D.E. Round	*U* H.W. Austin/ Mrs D.C. Shepherd-Barron	3/6, 6/4, 6/0
1935	F.J. Perry/ Miss D.E. Round	*U* H.C. Hopman/ Mrs H.C. Hopman	7/5, 4/6, 6/2
1936	F.J. Perry/ Miss D.E. Round	J.D. Budge/ Mrs S. P. Fabyan	7/9, 7/5, 6/4
1937	J.D. Budge/ Miss A. Marble	Y. Petra/ Mrs R. Mathieu	6/4, 6/1
1938	J.D. Budge/ Miss A. Marble	H. Henkel/ Miss S.P. Fabyan	6/1, 6/4
1939	R.L. Riggs/ Miss A. Marble	*U* F.H.D. Wilde/ Miss N.B. Brown	9/7, 6/1
1940–45	No competition		

	Champions	Runners-up	Score
1946	T. Brown/ Miss A.L. Brough	G.E. Brown/ Miss D. Bundy	6/4, 6/4
1947	J.E. Bromwich/ Miss A.L. Brough	C.F. Long/ Mrs N.M. Bolton	1/6, 6/4, 6/2
1948	J.E. Bromwich/ Miss A.L. Brough	F.A. Sedgman/ Miss D.J. Hart	6/2, 3/6, 6/3
1949	E.W. Sturgess/ Mrs S.P. Summers	J.E. Bromwich/ Miss A.L. Brough	9/7, 9/11, 7/5
1950	E.W. Sturgess/ Miss A. L. Brough	G.E. Brown/ Mrs P.C. Todd	11/9, 1/6, 6/4
1951	F.A. Sedgman/ Miss D.J. Hart	U M.G. Rose/ Mrs N.M. Bolton	7/5, 6/2
1952	F.A. Sedgman/ Miss D.J. Hart	U E. Morea/ Mrs T.D. Long	4/6, 6/3, 6/4
1953	E.V. Seixas/ Miss D.J. Hart	E. Morea/ Miss S.J. Fry	9/7, 7/5
1954	E.V. Seixas/ Miss D.J. Hart	K.R. Rosewall/ Mrs W. du Pont	5/7, 6/4, 6/3
1955	E.V. Seixas/ Miss D.J. Hart	E. Morea/ Miss A.L. Brough	8/6, 2/6, 6/3
1956	E.V. Seixas/ Miss S.J. Fry	G. Mulloy/ Miss A. Gibson	2/6, 6/2, 7/5
1957	M.G. Rose/ Miss D.R. Hard	N.A. Fraser/ Miss A. Gibson	6/4, 7/5
1958	R.N. Howe/ Miss L. Coghlan	K. Nielsen/ Miss A. Gibson	6/3, 13/11
1959	R.G. Laver/ Miss D.R. Hard	N.A. Fraser/ Miss M.E. Bueno	6/4, 6/3
1960	R.G. Laver/ Miss D.R. Hard	R.N. Howe/ Miss M.E. Bueno	13/11, 3/6, 8/6
1961	F.S. Stolle/ Miss L.R. Turner	R.N. Howe/ Miss E. Buding	11/9, 6/2
1962	N.A. Fraser/ Mrs W. du Pont	U R.D. Ralston/ Miss A.S. Haydon	2/6, 6/3, 13/11
1963	G K.N. Fletcher/ G Miss M. Smith	U R.A.J. Hewitt/ Miss D.R. Hard	11/9, 6/4
1964	F.S. Stolle/ Miss L.R. Turner	K.N. Fletcher/ Miss M. Smith	6/4, 6/4
1965	K.N. Fletcher/ Miss M. Smith	U A.D. Roche/ Miss J.A.M. Tegart	12/10, 6/3
1966	K.N. Fletcher/ Miss M. Smith	R.D. Ralston/ Mrs L.W. King	4/6, 6/3, 6/3
1967	G O.K. Davidson/ Mrs L.W. King	K.N. Fletcher/ Miss M.E. Bueno	7/5, 6/2
1968	K.N. Fletcher/ Mrs B.M. Court	U A. Metreveli/ Miss O. Morozova	6/1, 14/12
1969	F.S. Stolle/ Mrs P.F. Jones	A.D. Roche/ Mrs J.A.M. Tegart	6/2, 6/3
1970	U I. Nastase/ Miss R. Casals	U A. Metreveli/ Miss O. Morozova	6/3, 4/6, 9/7
1971	O.K. Davidson/ Mrs L.W. King	M.C. Riessen/ Mrs B.M. Court	3/6, 6/2, 15/13
1972	I. Nastase/ Miss R. Casals	K.G. Warwick/ Miss E.F. Goolagong	6/4, 6/4
1973	O.K. Davidson/ Mrs L.W. King	U R. Ramirez/ Miss J.S. Newberry	6/3, 6/2
1974	O.K. Davidson/ Mrs L.W. King	U M.J. Farrell/ Miss L.W. Charles	6/3, 9/7
1975	M.C. Riessen/ Mrs B.M. Court	U A.J. Stone/ Miss B.F. Stove	6/4, 7/5

	Champions	Runners-up	Score
1976	A.D. Roche/ Miss F. Durr	U R.L. Stockton/ Miss R. Casals	6/3, 2/6, 7/5

NB: Open Championships began in 1968.

WHO IS THE GREATEST?

Who has been the greatest player to appear on Wimbledon's Centre Court? A question often asked but impossible to answer with anything near certainty. A man like F.R. Burrow, whose experience spanned fifty of the early years of the Championships, gave only a qualified answer – and that with a humility that he did not always show.

He was a man used to weighing the odds, comparing performances and assessing strengths, yet he was very cautious in coming to his well-reasoned conclusions. They were that, up to 1936, the two greatest players were Laurie Doherty and Tilden and, he felt, had the two met at an equidistant time out of their own peak periods, Doherty would just have won.

Few post-war pundits would agree with Burrow, but how much is that because they never saw Doherty and because the higher tempo and demands of the modern game weigh heavily in the scale of their opinion? In *The Encyclopedia of Tennis* 1974, Allison Danzig, Harry Hopman and Lance Tingay all give Tilden first place, while Laurie Doherty gets one 8th and one 9th in their lists. Tilden himself said Cochet was the best ever.

I am not going to attempt an overall assessment but rather give my impressions of the players I have seen in the last thirty years. As a radio commentator on the game, impressions and trying to convey them to the listener are my business – so here goes.

Imagine all the post-war Wimbledon quarter-finalists (100), all at the peak of their prowess. Put them all in a grand draw for the Champion of champions. For a bit of spice add a hot pepper – Gonzales, whose great years were in the pro ranks. Who would dare to do the seeding?

But consider. There is no lack of champion spark or killer instinct or ability in that lot. So what will the winner need? He must survive seven rounds much tougher than any he has played in succession before – and he must have *flair*. There is only one man I would have staked my money on in that situation, Lew Hoad – Hoad, as strong as a tiger and gifted beyond measure. He needed the stimulus of a great occasion to rouse him from the casual attitude his tremendous talents allowed. As his opponent in that Wimbledon Final I would have expected to see – not Laver but Gonzales. What a magnificent match that would have been.

And of the women? My money would be on the girl who was never beaten at Wimbledon – Maureen Connolly. In her three-year reign Little Mo showed over and over again that she had the ability and fighting quality to raise her game whenever needed. In a similar post-war field (85) – with all at their developed best (and she, alas, was cut short by her riding accident) – I think she would have beaten each and every one.

So, very fearfully, I give you my lists – my impressions: *Men:* 1. Hoad; 2. Gonzales; 3. Laver; 4. Kramer; 5. Sedgman; 6. Rosewall; 7. Connors; 8. Borg; 9. Trabert; 10. Newcombe. *Women:* 1. Connolly; 2. King; 3. Betz; 4. Bueno; 5. Brough; 6. Hart; 7. Court; 8. Dupont; 9. Gibson; 10. Evert; 11. Goolagong.

Connors, Borg, Evert and Goolagong have not yet fully developed and all are likely to move up their respective ladders.

The two players who have given me the greatest pleasure to watch are Ken Rosewall and Maria Bueno. Maria at her best was for me the ultimate in tennis perfection.

100 men quarter-finalists and 85 women in the same 31 years suggests that it was 17·65% more difficult for a man to reach the quarter-finals and that therefore the general level of excellence in the men's field was higher. I realize that the women's draw is half a round less than the men's, but I do not believe this materially affects the percentage, though the drain of top men to the pros does.

SHORTEST FINAL

1881	*Men*	20 games:	W. Renshaw bt J.T. Hartley 6/0, 6/1, 6/1
1936	*Men*	20 games:	F.J. Perry bt G. von Cramm (suffering from a pulled muscle) 6/1, 6/1, 6/0
1911	*Women*	12 games:	D. Lambert Chambers bt D. Boothby 6/0, 6/0

LONGEST FINAL

1954	*Men*	58 games:	J. Drobny bt K.R. Rosewall 13/11, 4/6, 6/2, 9/7
1970	*Women*	46 games:	M. Court bt B.J. King 14/12, 11/9
1902	*Women*	53 games:	M.E. Robb bt C. Sterry 4/6, 13/11; rain held up play, match replayed next day 7/5, 6/1

LONGEST SINGLES MATCH

1969	*Men*	112 games:	R.A. Gonzales bt C. Pasarell 22/24, 1/6, 16/14, 6/3, 11/9 in the first round
1948	*Women*	54 games:	A. Weiwers bt O. Anderson 8/10, 14/12, 6/4 in the second round

LONGEST DOUBLES MATCH

1966	*Men*	98 games:	E.L. Scott/M. Pilic bt G.C. Richey/T. Ulrich 19/21, 12/10, 6/4, 4/6, 9/7 in the first round.
1933	*Women*	48 games:	P. Brazier/I.H. Wheatcroft bt M.E. Nonweiler/B. Soames 11/9, 5/7, 9/7 in the first round.

LONGEST MIXED DOUBLES MATCH

1967	56 games:	K.N. Fletcher/M.E. Bueno bt A. A. Metreveli/A. Dmitrieva 6/8, 7/5, 16/14 in the quarter-finals

TWICE OR MORE FINALISTS WITHOUT WINNING

Men:

F.L. Riseley	1903, 1904, 1906
H. Roper Barrett	1908, 1911
H.W. Austin	1932, 1938
G. von Cramm	1935, 1936, 1937
K. Nielsen	1953, 1955
K.R. Rosewall	1954, 1956, 1970, 1974
F.S. Stolle	1963, 1964, 1965
I. Nastase	1972, 1976

Women:

A.M. Morton	1908, 1909
E. Ryan	1921, 1930
L. de Alvarez	1926, 1927, 1928
D.R. Hard	1957, 1959

HIGHEST NUMBER OF SINGLES WINS

Men:

W. Renshaw	7 times	1881–6, 1889
H.L. Doherty	5 times	1902–6
R.F. Doherty	4 times	1897/1900
A.F. Wilding	4 times	1910–13
*R. Laver	4 times	1961–2, 1968–9

* All won after Challenge Round was abolished.

Women:

H. Wills Moody	8 times	1927–30, 1932–3, 1935, 1938
D. Lambert Chambers	7 times	1903–4, 1906, 1910–11 & 1913–14
B. Hillyard	6 times	1886, 1889, 1894, 1897, 1899/1900
S. Lenglen	6 times	1919–23, 1925
*B.J. King	6 times	1966–8, 1972–3, 1975
C. Sterry	5 times	1895–6, 1898, 1901, 1908
*L. Brough	4 times	1948–50, 1955

Youngest Winners

YEAR FIRST WON	MEN	EXACT AGE IN YEARS & DAYS	YEAR FIRST WON	WOMEN	EXACT AGE IN YEARS & DAYS
1891	W. Baddeley	19.174	1887	L. Dod	15.285
1931	S.B. Wood	19.243	1952	M. Connolly	17.291
1976	B. Borg	20.27	1905	M. Sutton	18.286
1881	W. Renshaw	20.191	1974	C.M. Evert	19.196
1932	H.E. Vines	20.278	1962	K. Susman	19.208
1925	R. Lacoste	21.2	1959	M.E. Bueno	19.266
1939	R.L. Riggs	21.132	1884	M. Watson	19.284
1956	L.A. Hoad	21.225	1971	E. Goolagong	19.337
1958	A.J. Cooper	21.291	1919	S. Lenglen	20.42
1974	J.S. Connors	21.307	1963	M. Smith	20.357
			1927	H. Wills	21.269

Oldest Winners

YEAR FIRST WON	MEN	EXACT AGE IN YEARS & DAYS	YEAR FIRST WON	WOMEN	EXACT AGE IN YEARS & DAYS
1909	A.W. Gore	41.183	1908	C. Sterry	37.281
1930	W.T. Tilden	37.145	1900	B. Hillyard	36.242
1914	N.E. Brookes	36.235	1914	D. Lambert Chambers	35.304
1887	H.F. Lawford	36.53			
1954	J. Drobny	32.263	1912	E.W. Larcombe	33.27
1975	A. Ashe	31.360	1938	H. Wills Moody	32.269
1880	J.T. Hartley	31.187	1955	A.L. Brough	32.113
1969	R.G. Laver	30.331	1975	B.J. King	31.224
1946	Y. Petra	30.119	1958	A. Gibson	30.314
			1969	A. Jones	30.260

In her famous Challenge Round defence against Suzanne Lenglen in 1919, Mrs Lambert Chambers at 8/10, 6/4, 6/5, 40–15 had 2 match-points to become the oldest woman to win the title. She was then 40 years and 304 days old.

Oldest Finalists

YEAR	MEN	AGE	YEAR	WOMEN	AGE
1912	A.W. Gore	44.188	1920	D. Lambert Chambers	41.302
1974	K.R. Rosewall	39.246	1930	E. Ryan	38.149

MAIDEN NAMES OF MARRIED CHAMPIONS IN CHRONOLOGICAL ORDER

Mrs G.W. Hillyard	=	Miss Blanche Bingley
Mrs A. Sterry	=	Miss Chattie Cooper
Mrs Lambert Chambers	=	Miss Dolly Douglas
Mrs D.R. Larcombe	=	Miss Ethel Thompson
Mrs L.A. Godfree	=	Miss Kitty McKane
Mrs F.S. Moody	=	Miss Helen Wills
Mrs J.R. Susman	=	Miss Karen Hanze
Mrs L.W. King	=	Miss Billy Jean Moffitt
Mrs P.F. Jones	=	Miss Ann Haydon
Mrs B.M. Court	=	Miss Margaret Smith

RECORD ATTENDANCES

1967 First time 300,000 exceeded for the Fortnight
1975 388,591 – record for the Fortnight
1975 Friday 27 June: 37,290 – record for *one* day.

The gates have been closed 6 times since the last war.

Play has gone into the third week in the following years
1912 1919 1922 1930 1963 1972

Centre Court has 10,651 seats and standing room for nearly 3000
No. 1 Court has 5100 seats and standing room for nearly 1500

SINGLES TITLES BY WINNING NATIONS

	MEN				*WOMEN*				
	Pre 1914	*1919–39*	*1946–76*	*Sub-total*	*Pre 1914*	*1919–39*	*1946–76*	*Sub-total*	**Total**
GB	32(13)	3(1)		35(14)	29(9)	4(2)	2(2)	35(13)	**70(27)**
USA		9(6)	12(12)	21(18)	2(1)	10(3)	22(10)	34(14)	**55(32)**
A'lia	2(1)	3(2)	14(7)	19(10)			4(2)	4(2)	**23(12)**
NZ	4(1)			4(1)				6(1)	**4(1)**
France		6(3)	1(1)	7(4)		6(1)			**13(5)**
G'many						1(1)		1(1)	**1(1)**
Egypt			1(1)	1(1)					**1(1)**
Brazil							3(1)	3(1)	**3(1)**
Spain			1(1)	1(1)					**1(1)**
Cz'kia			1(1)	1(1)					**1(1)**
Sweden			1(1)	1(1)					**1(1)**

NB: Figures in brackets show number of champions.

COMPOSITION OF THE DRAW

	1914		*1939*		*1976*	
	Men	*Woman*	*Men*	*Women*	*Men*	*Women*
Number in Draw	102	51	128	96	128	96
Number of Nations	8	3	24	15	29	20
GB	88	47	56	68	14	16
USA	1	1	6	5	33	32
A'lia	3	0	2	0	21	11
France	2	2	4	4	5	2
Germany	5	1	5	3	5	2
Rest of World	3	0	55	16	50	33

The All England Club

Highest Number of Wimbledon Titles

19 Elizabeth Ryan (12 Doubles, 7 Mixed Doubles)
19 Billy Jean King (6 Singles, 9 Doubles, 4 Mixed Doubles)

Longest Interval Between First and Last Title

MEN:	WOMEN:
W. T. Tilden 10 years 1920–30	B. Hillyard 14 years 1886–1900
	H. Wills Moody 11 years 1927–38

Longest Interval Between First and Last Appearance in a Final

MEN:	WOMEN:
K. R. Rosewall 20 years 1954–74	C. Sterry 17 years 1895–1912
	D. K. Lambert Chambers 17 years 1903–20